WORK
Smart
NOT
HARD

George Sullivan

A FIRESIDE BOOK

Published by Simon & Schuster Inc.

New York   London   Toronto   Sydney   Tokyo

First Fireside Edition, 1988

Published by the Simon & Schuster Trade Division
by arrangement with Facts on File, Inc.
Simon & Schuster Building
Rockefeller Center
1230 Avenue of the Americas
New York, New York 10020

FIRESIDE and colophon are registered trademarks
of Simon & Schuster Inc.

Designed by Barbara Marks Graphic Design
Manufactured in the United States of America

10   9   8   7   6   5   4   3   2   1   Pbk.

Library of Congress Cataloging in Publication Data
Sullivan, George, date.
    Work smart, not hard.
    A Fireside Book.
    Includes bibliographies and index.
    1. Performance.   2. Labor productivity.   3. Planning.
I. Title.
HF5549.5.P35S85   1988   658.3'14   88-4607
ISBN 0-671-66801-3 Pbk.

Acknowledgments

Special thanks are due Midge, of course, for all her help (Wow!), and John Devaney, Don Wigal, Kay O'Reilly, Gina Henry and Betsy Ryan.

Contents

Introduction

~~~~~~

Shirley Zussman, a sex and marital therapist in New York City, is from the generation of young professionals who entered the job market after World War II. She finds striking differences between the professionals of her day and those embarked on careers today.

"These young people want to make it earlier and they work harder for it," she says. "I can't believe

the number of hours they work. Spending ten or twelve hours a day and even weekends at the office is not unusual. One of my patients who works for a large law firm says he can never go back to his office in the evening or on a Sunday morning without finding many people there."

There's an enormous peer pressure to acquire the symbols of success, says Zussman, a former president of the American Association of Sex Educators, Counselors and Therapists. But it's more than that. "There seems to be no limit to the demands from their employers," she says. "Workaholism seems almost to be expected from employees. There's also a great deal of travel that's required. A lot of couples seem to be saying 'Hi' to one another in passing."

Zussman says that she and other sex therapists and family counselors are getting complaints from more and more young couples that their marriages are suffering because both partners are worn out from their love affair with success. "A lot of them say they have little or no time for sex," she reports. "There's a feeling that they're not even interested, that sex has become yet another chore, and that this is disturbing to them because they are the kind of people who 'want it all.' "

Zussman says some of these young people sound like people in their mid-40s or 50s. "They're asking questions such as, 'When am I going to start enjoying myself?' " All of the striving for success isn't bringing the rewards and satisfaction they've expected.

"What they have to do," explains Zussman, "sounds very easy but is very hard to do. They have to step back and look at their lives; they have to ask themselves, 'Is this what I want?' The solutions don't come easily. This may be a generation that is just going to have to pay a high price."

THE HARD WORK SYNDROME

Hard work and professional success are inalterably linked in the American psyche. "Plough deep while sluggards sleep," Benjamin Franklin wrote. And he offered countless tips on how to use time efficiently, e.g., "Never leave till tomorrow that which you can do today." Everyone has heard of the benefits to be derived from putting one's shoulder to the wheel and keeping one's nose to the grindstone. Edison observed that "Genius is one percent inspiration and ninety-nine percent perspiration."

Such axioms were hooted at during the 1960s, when many young people seemed to prefer dropping out to traditional success. But during the decade that followed, the majority of young people again began striving for success.

Two painful recessions during the early 1980s served to raise the anxiety level. Today the obsession to climb the career ladder, to get in the fast lane, may begin even before a child enters school.

People everywhere are searching for some secret formula that is going to help them make it big. *The Subject Guide to Books in Print* lists more than 700 titles dealing with success and how to achieve it. In addition to such standard books as *What It Takes to Get to the Top and Stay There* or *Success Through a Positive Mental Attitude,* there are titles that suggest that it's swell to bend the rules, e.g., *Getting Yours, Winning with Deception and Bluff* and *How to Get Ahead by "Psyching Out" Your Boss and Co-Workers.*

The pressure is so great that some feel compelled to cheat. Companies such as Fidelifacts are proof of that. With offices in 17 cities, Fidelifacts verifies backgrounds of job applicants. The company has found that resumes contain questionable information in about 30 percent of all cases. A master's degree that was never earned will be cited. Or an individual will claim to have worked longer for a firm than was actually the case in an effort to conceal a period of unemployment.

But the most widespread manifestation of the drive for success is stress, considered by many authorities to be the major adult health problem today. According to the American Academy of Family Physicians, two-thirds of all office visits to family doctors are triggered by stress-related symptoms. Costs to industry are estimated at $150 billion a year, says the American Stress Institute.

Long-term stress can cause physical and emotional exhaustion ending in burnout, which *Time* magazine has called "a syndrome verging on a trend." The air-traffic controllers went on a strike in 1981, at least in part, because of burnout. William McGuire, president of the National Education Association, has said that burnout among teachers "threatens to reach hurricane force if it isn't checked soon." Students burn out. Housewives burn out. Executives burn out.

WORKING SMART, DOING MORE

Not everyone ends up disillusioned, engulfed in unhappiness or overcome by stress. Plenty of successful people love what they do. They have tremendous enthusiasm for their jobs, a feeling of always being in control and yearning to be challenged.

The difference often lies in working less and accomplishing more. That's what this book is about. It examines the crucial skills that successful men and women possess and gives advice on how to develop them. These skills frequently have to do with organization, that is, with putting one's life in order, deciding upon career and personal goals and taking the steps necessary to achieve them. They have to do with managing or avoiding stress, working happily and productively with both superiors and equals and delegating to those who work for you, making the most of your time on the job and getting the most out of leisure. These skills also involve becoming more effective and efficient.

Effectiveness and efficiency are not to be taken as ends in themselves, however. Michael Korda, corporate vice-president and editor-in-chief at Simon & Schuster, has expressed that thought in these terms: "A system that merely frees someone to send out 100 'reminder memos' a day instead of 50 is not productive of anything but reminder memos."

Says Korda: "Most 'time-efficiency' enthusiasts are simply wearing themselves out to cram more trivia into the day. It's true they may save a minute or two by scrawling a 'yes' or a 'no' at the bottom of a letter and returning it, rather than writing or dictating a reply—but the *real* time saving question is, What are you going to do with the time saved, in a larger sense?"

Working smart means more than merely becoming a winner in terms of your job or career by putting more time in your life. It means improving relationships with your family and friends and developing a sense of mental and physical well-being. It means learning to live your life to the fullest, enjoying the richness and reward that each day brings.

1

Who Wins; Who Doesn't

~~~~~~

Everyone wants to win. Winning means getting what you want, your fantasy. Maybe you want to own a big Rolls Royce, a home in Malibu or write a mystery novel. Maybe you want to join the cast of an afternoon soap or become board chairman at Sperry Rand.

"Experts" agree that there is no best way to realize your fantasy, to win. There is no step-by-step

formula. But there are critical skills that almost all winners manifest. Probably no one has them all. They exist in pieces and parts,
right along with a panoply of weaknesses.

But winners develop most of these skills to a high degree,
whether intentionally or not. In other words, they do not leave
winning to chance. They pursue it; they make winning happen.

The qualities that help ensure success include:

THE SUCCESS MINDSET

People who eventually make it big have a winning attitude. They
have enthusiasm for their work. They always act as if their job or
profession is the key element in the realization of their ultimate.
It's almost as if they are working for themselves.

In stressful situations, winners have no doubts about themselves. They don't start questioning themselves and seeking alternative courses. They're tenacious; they persevere.

There's pride and self-esteem involved, too. Behavioral scien-
tists have found that successful men and women have both a desire
for and expectation of success. Those who fail to achieve often
have the desire but lack expectation.

"A truly successful person knows early on in the game that he
or she is going to succeed," says John Fanning, president and chief
executive officer of Uniforce, a national temporary-help firm.
"The only question is when. Winners look at adversities as challenges. To them, opportunities come disguised as problems."

But you can overdo. "People sometimes come to us with an
over-inflated image of themselves and their ability," Fanning adds.
"In the interview, when we ask, 'What are your shortcomings?'
they're dumbfounded. They feel they have no weaknesses. We
want people who are self-confident but who also have a realistic
understanding of their capabilities. We don't want them thinking,
'You need me,' or 'I'm indispensable.' "

SETTING GOALS

Winners are single-minded in pursuing well-defined goals. Setting goals means planning. And winning won't happen unless you've planned for it.

You should have a main goal, a career goal, that lies five or ten years in the future. It should involve something more than a good salary, an easy commute or lavish perks. It should be something you want to accomplish, not something you think you can accomplish.

If you don't set a career goal and work toward it, chance and circumstance are going to determine where you go. It should be the other way around, of course; your goals should determine what direction you take.

You should also have short-range goals, those that apply to today, tomorrow, next week and next month. Achieving your short-range goals enables you to attain your long-range goals.

Having goals increases your efficiency and effectiveness. It's easier for you to make decisions. And the greater your desire to achieve your goals, the more efficient and effective you will be.

Think of your goals in terms of a "mission," advises Robert Moscowitz in *How to Organize Your Work and Your Life.* Says Moscowitz: "A military word, 'mission' connotes a degree of seriousness and dedication that has been washed out of the word 'goals' through overuse."

THE EDUCATIONAL ADVANTAGE

Education is one qualification that almost always pays rich dividends in terms of winning. Statistics show that the more education one has, the more money one is likely to earn. This chart, from the October 1985 issue of *Working Woman* magazine, shows the percentage of men and women of various education levels who have incomes of $30,000 or more a year.

Income $30,000+

EDUCATION	MEN	WOMEN
High school	48%	19%
College graduate	60	39
Graduate school	68	45
MBA	91	84
PhD, MD, LLB	83	62

Interestingly, the chart also makes it clear that educational de-grees for women are relatively more valuable than for men. With each step up the educational ladder, women increase their income more than men do. (The chart also shows that men, on the average, still earn more than women.)

While attending school gives one a significant edge, some schools give a bigger edge than others. In law, the magic names include Harvard, Yale, Columbia, Michigan, Chicago, Stanford, Northwestern, Duke and Virginia. For training in the practice of engineering, the leaders include Illinois, Purdue, Georgia Tech and Texas A & M. For opening doors in a career as a research engineer, it's California Institute of Technology, Stanford, University of California, Berkeley, and MIT.

By the mid-1980s, recruiters were beginning to say that a mas-ter's degree in business administration (MBA) had lost some of its importance as a means of vaulting men and women toward cor-porate leadership. One reason was the proliferation of new business programs, some of which were being offered by schools with less than glittering reputations. However, holders of MBA's from such schools as Harvard, Stanford, Wharton, Northwestern, Dart-mouth and Chicago were still in heavy demand.

"Think of the MBA as a credential," says Kevin Daley, presi-dent of Communispond, a leading firm in teaching executives communications skills. "If you're competing in a company where there are a good number of people on the same level as you are, and you're constantly reaching for something that puts you ahead of those with whom you're competing, that something could be an MBA. In such a situation, you could be at a disadvantage without it."

CONTROLLING OTHERS

In order to be successful, people need other people, or at least need to know how to deal effectively with other people. Some people do it intuitively. With others, it's an acquired skill.

Either way, there's nothing Machiavellian about it. It's simply give and take between individuals. High achievers really care about their colleagues and subordinates. They know what makes them tick. They know how to use a person's goals and desires to help achieve their own goals.

Successful people don't take anyone or anything for granted. They're quick to show appreciation. They're good listeners. They're perfectly willing to let the speaker be the "star," even though they have a more interesting story to tell. It's the Merv Griffin technique of listening.

They avoid head-on collisions with people. They realize that a heated argument accomplishes nothing and the damage wrought may never be repaired. In other words, they deny themselves the pleasure of getting angry. No matter what, they stay calm and reasonable—in control.

Some people try to gain control of others by playing hardball. Don't! *Psychology Today* once studied 21 derailed executives, successful people who had been expected to go even higher in the organization but who, after reaching a plateau, were fired or forced to retire early. These individuals were compared with 20 "arrivers," people who made it all the way to the executive suite. Those who failed to fulfill their potential were usually victimized by a combination of personality qualities and external circumstances, but the one flaw many had in common was an insensitivity to others.

Playing hardball can also imply an abrasive, bullying style. It's being cold, aloof and arrogant. It's pushing subordinates to the very limit. It's taking credit for other people's work and blaming other people for one's mistakes.

Executives who play rough find that people no longer wish to work with them. They stop getting invited to intimate tête-à-têtes. Their information sources dry up. Their support base gets destroyed.

It's trite but true; success depends on following the adage: "Do unto others as you would have them do unto you." *Working Woman* magazine put it this way: "Being a bitch doesn't pay off, but neither does being a martyr. Successful people treat themselves and other people well."

PLAYING THE PART

Your personal appearance, how you articulate your ideas and how you project yourself are critical factors. In many firms, the "boardroom presence" can be as important as being related to the boss, perhaps even more important.

You must dress in a manner that bespeaks success. Sure, there are successful people who dress as if they had picked up their clothes from the bedroom floor that morning, but such individuals are a great rarity today. Never underestimate the importance of grooming and fashion.

Playing the part also means having the ability to present ideas clearly and with authority. Maybe this means you should take a course in public speaking. In a national poll taken not long ago, the number one fear among the public was revealed to be not fear of death, not fear of heights, but fear of talking in front of a large group. You have to rid yourself of any such feeling. Fortunately, you can do so and learn to articulate your ideas clearly and decisively through courses offered by private business schools and public school adult-education programs.

Supervisors and managers need communication skills in dealing with the people who work for them. Such skills render any type of one-on-one encounter more productive (as when you're asking for a raise, for instance). Executives require such skills to be able to deliver effective speeches. They're helpful in media interviews or when appearing before congressional committees.

Communication skills are vital when making presentations. "In the old days you could be a 'numbers man' and weave your way in, and be silent. But it's different today," says Kevin Daley. "You won't make it today unless you're a good presenter." Daley likes to quote Harry Holiday, former board chairman of Armco, Inc., who said: "I've never known a major capital investment to be approved by the board of directors on the basis of the numbers alone. It was also their sense of the individual and their confidence in the individual making the recommendation that caused them to make that decision."

In terms of getting ahead today, there are few things as important as the ability to communicate. One reason is that many business executives are engulfed in paper. And most of the reports, memorandums and all the rest are poorly written. They thus prefer verbal communication. Besides being more efficient, it enables business people to size up the individual making the pitch.

"Facts don't move the world," Kevin Daley says. "Feelings do. It's your feelings about the facts that I present that will cause you to decide yes or no. The feelings are governed by the impact of me upon you. Or, to put it another way—your evaluation of me standing behind those facts. So if I am thoroughly confident, and my numbers are set up properly, and I give you the feeling of confidence, then you'll buy it. But even if the numbers stand up properly, but I don't appear confident, you'll be suspicious, you won't buy."

Daley remembers the years when he was in charge of new business at J. Walter Thompson, the biggest advertising agency at the time. "The prospective client would come in, and we'd make a presentation," he recalls. "The client would be exposed to three or four other agencies. Now, what were the differences? You'd think the differences were in the sample commercials we'd all show, or in the print ads. Well, relatively speaking, they were all about the same. The prospect would end up buying a *sense* of wanting to work with one group of people as opposed to the other groups. That's presentation skill."

. . . . .

Suggested Reading

Dare to Change, by Joe Alexander (Signet, 1984). Practical tips for making your future better than your past.

How to Get Whatever You Want Out of Life, by Dr. Joyce Brothers (Ballantine, 1985). How to achieve love, power, riches, success and a good marriage.

The Complete Book of Success; Your Guide to Becoming a Winner, by Renee Harmon (Prentice-Hall, 1984). Step-by-step guidelines for making decisions, managing stress and reaching your goals.

How to Win Friends and Influence People, by Dale Carnegie (Pocket Books, 1982). More than 15 million copies sold since 1936; updated for the 1980s.

Wishcraft; How to Get What You Really Want, by Barbara Sher with Annie Gottlieb (Ballantine, 1979). Original and practical advice on pinpointing goals and making dreams come true.

ADVICE FROM EXPERTS

Success has many other ingredients. One's IQ and family background can be important. The willingness to take risks is certainly a factor, that is, the desire to abandon a previous level of accomplishment—a "comfort zone," as one expert calls it—for something loftier. Successful people also have a tendency to solve problems rather than assess blame. They recognize the impossibility of perfection and the probability of success for a job done well. As management consultant and author James K. Van Fleet puts it, "A successful person always acts as if it were impossible to fail." And they back up their positive attitudes with commitment, persistence, and enjoyment of what they do. "I had a good idea and I gave it everything I had," said cookie king Famous Amos. "I had to go all the way."

In the pages that follow, individuals who have analyzed the

attitudes and behaviors of successful men and women, plus a number of actual achievers, set forth their thoughts on what makes a successful person. Some stress personal qualities, others point to timing and teamwork, and one expert insists that support from others takes precedence over persistence and attitude. That the experts differ only proves that there is no single path: everyone to some extent invents the rules and makes them work for him or herself.

·····

James K. Van Fleet

Management consultant; lecturer; author, *Twenty-Five Steps to Power & Mastery Over People* (Prentice-Hall, 1983).

Successful people live by two maxims:

They do the thing they fear to do, and by so doing gain the power to do it.

A successful person always acts as if it were impossible to fail.

·····

K. J. Kriggy

Chairman of the board and chief executive officer, Wilson Foods Corp.

A number of capabilities and attributes play an important role in achieving success in any endeavor. This could include planning, organization, motivation, determination, priority setting, perseverance and, certainly, talent. The most important qualities which are key to success, however, are personal integrity and the ability to work with people. No lasting success can be achieved without this foundation.

. . . . .

J. Peter Grace

Chairman and chief executive officer, W. R. Grace & Co.

Working hard *is* working smart. A commitment to hard work, in my judgment, is the main characteristic of those who move up the job ladder quickly.

Beyond that, let me share a few other observations:

> Successful people are operations-oriented and profit-motivated. The more they want success and its associated rewards, the faster they can get it.
>
> Vision is essential. In business, those who can identify future profit centers in which a company can establish niche markets with proprietary products/technology, commanding large market shares, are the winners.
>
> Organization, systems and standardization pay off. I've heard about the neat desk symbolizing the hobgoblin of small minds, but the fact is that moving up requires taking on ever-increasing responsibilities. Without the management organizational capacity to prevent it, important opportunities fall through the cracks and breakdowns occur.
>
> Successful people are smart and come across that way. Seeing that quality in others is almost an intuitive judgment.
>
> People who make it are tough and independent. They typify the American values at the core of successful capitalism: They don't follow the herd, they are fiercely individualistic, and they are skeptical—even of themselves.

. . . . .

Robert L. Shook

Business executive; author, *The Ten Greatest Salespersons* (Harper & Row, 1978), *The Entrepreneurs* (Harper & Row,

1980), *The Chief Executive Officers* (Harper & Row, 1981), *The Perfect Sales Presentation* (Bantam Books, 1986).

Big corporations in America are structured to develop management candidates from within. It's viewed as a sign of failure when a company must go "outside" and bring in a high-ranking executive. It means that the company lacks the ability to produce its own brand of management. For instance, Thomas A. Murphy, past CEO of General Motors, began as a clerk in the accounting department. David W. Mitchell, who held the same position at Avon, started with the cosmetics company as a mailroom clerk. Robert L. Beck, Prudential's present CEO, started his career pounding the pavement in the field as a life insurance agent.

I've researched the lives of these and scores of other chief executive officers. Through extensive interviews, I learned that a single quality seems to have possessed each of them to move quickly up the corporate ladder. I call it *total commitment.*

Total commitment is something more than determination, dedication or drive. It's much broader in scope. The would-be athlete who is labeled "too small" or "too slow" and succeeds in spite of whatever shortcomings he or she might have has this winning quality. The thought of failing never enters one's mind.

Total commitment is also that extra resource that the individual draws upon whenever the challenge is great, the stakes are high, or defeat stares them in the face. It's the stuff that drives successful men and women to overcome the obstacles that defeat ordinary people.

· · · · ·

Madelyn P. Jennings

Senior vice president, personnel and administration, Gannett Company, Inc.

Achievers *always* have drive and they are tenacious because they know nothing works unless they do. The good ones also know how to encourage themselves and others. They don't think it's weak to sometimes be vulnerable. They know when to speak up and when to shut up. They know when to say yes, no and *wait*. They deliver beyond the obvious. And they're rarely bored. They accept the comical in themselves. They know a sense of humor is the last thing to lose.

If I were asked to give advice as to how to be a better achiever, here's what I'd say:

Listen better. Most people only listen about 20 percent of the time.

Move faster and

Think faster. You'd be amazed how much more is possible. Remember, right now you're probably using only about 5 percent of your brainpower.

Work for consensus in advance of presenting your great idea at a meeting.

Know that in all you do, reliability and service are the names of the game. People you can't count on are rarely achievers.

Keep asking: How can I do this better. Remember, the opposite of a great idea may also be a great idea.

Find out more about your company than just what your job demands. That helps you make more sense of things and be more valuable.

Be honest. Be ethical. How you play the game really is important. When I interview people, ethics and integrity are probably the first things I look for.

Have a short memory for mistakes—yours and others'.

Look to catch people doing something right; ask who's right and *what's* wrong.

Don't be a pushover. You have the right to be strong.

Get out if you don't like the kind of work you're in. It's a big world out there and you can start over more than one time.

Remember that while tyrants are bad so are soft supervisors. At Gannett, we talk about a philosophy of being "hard on performance, soft on people." That makes a lot of sense.

Take risks. I took a four-level demotion at one time—to achieve my goals. Every one of my closest friends advised me not to do so. I ignored them. I went with my gut. I happened to be right that time.

As Lily Tomlin says, "When it becomes comprehensible that reality is all you know, you know all you're going to know right now." Each of you must judge your own reality.

· · · · ·

David Asman

Editor, "The Manager's Journal," *The Wall Street Journal*

Whenever you look at really successful people in business, you see a whole string of events in which they displayed an exquisite sense of timing. They know when to capitalize on a situation; they know when to pull back. They recognize those key moments when that whisker of a difference really matters.

These people have the ability to sense when the market is crying out for a new product before anyone else has sensed it. And they also have the ability, after investing time and energy in a project, to realize that it's not going to make it, to let go.

It's much the same as being a good comedian, a Jack Benny. Benny's jokes weren't particularly funny. He didn't make faces or clown around. What made him great was his brilliant sense of timing. In music, there's Vladimir Horowitz. Watch him and you realize that ninety-nine percent of what he does is the same as what any other concert pianist does. But it's that one percent of feeling and timing that makes the difference, that makes Horowitz the pianist that no one else is.

There are countless examples in major corporations. One is Don Burr, chief executive officer at People Express Airlines. Burr always had the idea of building an airline that would offer fares cheap enough to enable people to use it like mass transit. The proper time to capitalize on that idea came in 1980 with airline deregulation, and that's when Burr made his move.

Donald Trump is another example. When everyone else was

giving up on the New York real estate scene, Trump jumped in. His sense of timing earned him incredible tax abatements. Trump was in the right place at the right time, but so were a helluva lot of other people. Nobody else capitalized on it.

It's really something within one's character. I think you can work to become more successful by following certain mechanical steps. But I don't think there's anything mechanistic about that sense of timing or "feel," and it's what separates the really successful from those that are merely competent.

· · · · ·

William Proxmire
U.S. Senator (Wisconsin)

What enables some individuals to climb quickly up the job ladder? I would suggest the following: First, motivation, strong motivation. Number two, persistence. Number three, an understanding of what it is the boss wants and needs. Number four, an ability to conciliate different viewpoints and arrive at a compromise that can be satisfactory for all those who have the authority to help achieve the common end.

· · · · ·

Ken Auletta
Columnist; author, *The Underclass* (Random House, 1983), *The Streets Were Paved with Gold: The Decline of New York—An American Tragedy* (Random House, 1980), *The Art of Corporate Success* (Penguin, 1985), *Greed & Glory on Wall Street: The Fall of the House of Lehman* (Random House, 1986)

My sense is that individuals have a series of qualities, not any single quality, that determines their success. Among them would be self confidence, the ability, even when you have not busted out and made a name for yourself, or have been recognized for possessing certain talents, to believe in yourself, and to wake up each morning and continue each day believing you're going to succeed, you're going to make a difference, believing that you've got some talent.

I found that to be true not only as it relates to corporations but I found that to be true when studying poverty. Oftentimes the difference between the person who succeeds in climbing out of poverty and the person who fails—often, not always—is the element of self confidence, belief in themselves.

This allows them to try situations, to venture forth from the house and say, "I've got to get off welfare, I can succeed, I'm afraid of this job interview I'm going out on but, dammit, I've got to do it. It's the only way out."

The same is true in a corporate situation, where an executive or would-be executive says, "I know this is risky for my company to do this. But, dammit, that's what we're in business to do, to grow, to make breakthroughs." The only way you can do that is by taking chances.

That's one quality. A second quality I saw is some sense of vision, which in a certain sense relates to the first quality, in that the individual has a sense of belief in something long range, be it a belief in a product that will eventually work, a belief that the company should not overdiversify, should really "stick to the knitting," as Peters and Waterman [*In Search of Excellence*] called it, which means sticking to what you know best as a company.

This relates to people in poverty circumstances, too. It means being able to say, "I'm going to go to school. I can't get diverted by my friends who want to hang out. I'm going to finish school, get my degree, go into job training—or whatever. That's my route out of this."

It's having a plan. And having the courage to stick to it, which is a kind of self confidence. It can be more than a plan. A really talented person will often have a vision of the future. That plan or vision cannot be shaken by quarterly returns or a profit picture that is not encouraging, or by any other short-term adversity.

A third quality is the ability to pick good people and in doing so not be afraid of talent. By this I mean you should surround yourself with people who are unafraid to tell you no, to talk back to you or to challenge your ideas. Rather than be threatened by that, you are nurtured by it. A large corporation cannot be built on the back of a single individual; it takes a team.

It's a rare individual who is comfortable with talent. People who you know want your job and who feel they can do it, can be very threatening.

A fourth quality is the ability to delegate. To pick quality people alone is not enough. There's no use having good people unless you give them some sense that they can make decisions on their own. And that they don't have to be messenger boys.

This comes back to self confidence. The more I talk about this, the single quality that becomes more important—and really has many ramifications—is self confidence.

. . . . .

Maynard M. Gordon

Publisher, editor, *Motor News Analysis*; author, *The Iacocca Management Technique* (Dodd, Mead, 1985)

How did Lee Iacocca, a self starter who became one of the auto industry's most celebrated "people movers" and motivators, make the quantum leap from being the son of immigrant parents to scaling the heights of American management?

It was more than his flamboyance and aggressiveness and his effective use of communications and public relations.

At Ford, Iacocca developed a "black book" system of vigil over all senior and junior executives. He kept aware of every staffer's performance through his own black book on the executives reporting to him. They in turn kept tabs on their own underlings. This system followed Iacocca's belief that "if you can't grade a man, you can't follow him at all." This technique of constantly reviewing and grading was linked to a requirement for setting and meeting quarterly goals.

When he arrived at Chrysler, Iacocca demonstrated his skills as a product developer and marketer par excellence. These qualities were in short supply at Chrysler at the time.

Iacocca also possessed an intensity in concentration not unlike that seen in a champion tennis player or diver. Such concentration in a leader can be magnified toward fellow workers, psychologists who study business executives believe, and often accomplishes results that others achieve only through coercive methods.

Leo Kelmenson, president of Kenyon & Eckhardt, Chrysler's ad agency, once called Iacocca a "profound leader who is absolutely dedicated in accomplishing whatever he has his mind on. He sets his course and attacks; if you get in his way, he'll run over you like an M-1 Tank."

. . . . .

Eleanor Rowe
▬▬▬▬▬▬▬▬▬▬▬

Author, *Waiting Games; How to Get Rich, Powerful, Sexy and Healthy While You're Killing Time!* (Facts On File, 1983)

Success emanates from some people. You can see it in their every move. It is like a self-intensifying aura.

A friend of ours owns and runs a multimillion-dollar computer software business. Eight years ago, as a strapped college student, he earned his room and board by taking care of our young sons. I remember telling him then that I was sure he would be very successful because of his attitude. He was enthusiastic and open to all opportunities. He saw value and found delight in people and situations that others failed to notice. And he never allowed himself to remain discouraged at a setback. If something wasn't a total success, at least it was a useful lesson.

To Famous Amos, the cookie king, failure is also an alien concept. He and I were guests together on the "Panorama" talk show in Washington, D.C. We waited in the green room with Jesse Jackson, the guest who was to precede us on the show. Not one to miss an opportunity, Amos talked with Reverend Jackson and gave him a package of his cookies. When Famous Amos was announced as the next guest, Jesse Jackson smiled and waved the cookies before the camera.

The subject of our segment was his success and what others could learn from it. The secret, he maintained, is in the power of

idea. "I had a good idea," he said, "and I gave it everything I had."
His accountant wanted him to start slowly and safely, to begin his
cookie operation out of his own kitchen. "No," he said, "I had to
go all the way—one-hundred percent."

I added that if you give any energy to the idea of failure, even
in your subconscious, you may draw it to yourself. Our minds
have that power. We create with our thoughts. The host pointed
out that Amos had been very lucky. For example, he had seen him
actively promoting that "luck." His last words on the show were,
"We create everything that happens in our lives."

This is ancient wisdom. In Buddhism, for example, you find as
a basic principle that "Everything is an emanation of Mind."

. . . . .

Jeffrey L. Seglin

Contributing editor, *Financial Planning* and *Goodlife*
magazines; personal finance writer, *Boston* magazine; editor,
Inc. and *Venture* magazines; author, *America's New Breed of
Entrepreneurs* (Acropolis Books, 1985)

In doing research for my book, I interviewed the heads of about
three hundred companies, companies that had been started from
scratch. I ended up discussing approximately fifty of these companies in the book.

These ranged from small to middle market firms, with annual
sales anywhere from $50,000 to $40,000,000, but most were
around $1,000,000 to $2,000,000.

These businesspeople all loved what they were doing. Even
though they worked real hard, it never seemed to them as if they
were working at all. They reminded me of my six-year-old
nephew. In 1985, when I took him to see a baseball game, I remember saying to him, "This could be the last baseball game we see for
a while because the players may be going out on strike." I explained to him that the players wanted a better contract, that is,
more money. He said, "You mean they get paid to play!" It was
not hard work for them. They just loved it so much. If anything,

it was hard work for them *not* to do what they were doing. That's a very common trait in successful people

From my work on the book, I developed six maxims of entrepreneurial marketing used by successful companies. The first had to do with product development. These people knew their market and gave it what it needed. I call this The Problem-Solving Approach.

Al Felly, who runs Felly's Flowers in Madison, Wisconsin, has the largest per capita flower sales in the nation for a metropolitan area. His marketing strategy is based on the concept that flowers cost too much and don't last long enough. "When flowers last longer," he says, "they cost less." Since he knew that flowers could be made to last longer if cut under water, Felly developed an underwater flower-cutting machine, which he now holds the patent on. It's being marketed to other florists and Felly gets a royalty on each sale. He's always testing flowers in different solutions in an effort to get them to last longer. He's full of tips. When I interviewed him, he told me that if you mix equal amounts of tap water and Seven-Up, or any other carbonated lemon–lime soda, and used it as a solution for flowers, you could double their life.

A second maxim I call The Entrepreneurial Difference. These businesspeople offer a product or service that is better than similar products or services. They give the consumer a little bit more bang for the buck. Rick Melman and his company, Lettuce Entertain You Enterprises, Inc., opened Ed Debevic's Short Orders/Deluxe, a theme diner, in Chicago late in 1984. Ed Debevic's bowling trophies decorate the place. A sign welcoming Ed back from the Korean War hangs on one wall. But Ed Debevic doesn't exist. He's a guy they created a history for.

The third maxim involves pinpointing the market and selling to it. It is what I called The Target Practice Proverb. Through the use of such techniques as direct mail software, low-power television or tunnel radio, these entrepreneurs target their specific markets and thus continue to draw business from them.

Fourth, is what I call The Presentation Principle. This has to do with the methods by which businesspeople cast their products or services in a favorable light. It can involve almost anything from an appealing company logo to a good-looking brochure. It frequently has to do with advertising, whether it be newspaper, television or direct mail.

The fifth and sixth maxims are The Open Throttle Theory and The Selling Code. These involve putting the first four maxims into effect—hitting the market with everything you've got.

You've got the product or services that solve the problem, you've got the entrepreneurial difference, you've targeted the market that wants what you have and you've instituted the presentation principle, and your product or service has the right look. Then you go after the market, selling often, selling hard.

. . . . .

Scott Witt
▶▶▶▶▶▶▶▶▶▶▶▶

Author, *How Self-Made Millionaires Build Their Fortunes* (Prentice-Hall, 1979), *How to Be Twice as Smart, Boosting Your Brainpower and Unleashing the Miracles of Your Mind* (Prentice-Hall, 1983)

What contributes to job success? Three of the most important qualities are self-confidence, self-assertiveness and self-promotion.

Self-confidence is achieved by knowing what you do best and concentrating on that, rather than going off on many different tangents.

Self-assertiveness is letting others know of your abilities in an ingratiating way. An effective technique: Find a need in your organization that is currently unmet, and then prove you are the best person to fill that need. Sometimes it's called creating your own turf. You take on a task no one else has handled (or perhaps even wanted to handle) and do it exceptionally well. I've seen many people achieve instant stardom in their organizations that way, and it's not long before they're called on for bigger and more rewarding assignments.

The most effective *self-promoters* are not the ones who go about boasting of their talents and achievements. Instead, they promote their *projects*. Nobody can fault you for that, and the good name you build for your project rubs off on you, the person. Lee Iacocca didn't go around boasting that he was going to save Chrysler. He went around asking everyone's *help* in saving Chrysler; that was the project. But when Chrysler was, indeed, saved, it was he who got the credit—not the government for making the loan, or the union for making concessions, or the customers for sticking with the product.

. . . . .

Peggy J. Berry

Author, *The Corporate Couple; Living the Corporate Game* (Franklin Watts, 1985)

Success is abstract, based on attitudes, perceptions, and evaluations as defined by the individual. Therefore, success as an attainment is variable and as such, I can give only the qualities I perceive as necessary to success as I define the term and the state. Through habit, I divide successful people into two categories: authoritative and charismatic.

Intelligence, knowledge, and job ability are the obvious basics of any kind of job success and many people have succeeded through sheer superiority and force of these strengths alone. I term such success as authoritative because these basic ingredients are deftly used in the acquisition and utilization of power. Familiar examples might include the "robber barons" (Jay Gould, J. P. Morgan, etc.), President Lyndon B. Johnson, Dan Rather (CBS News), Sam Donaldson (ABC News), Gloria Steinem (Editor, MS Magazine), and W. Michael Blumenthal (Chairman and Chief Executive Officer, Burroughs Corporation).

Compare the above examples to success stories such as Lee Iacocca (Chairman, Chrysler Corporation), Mary Kay Ash (Chairman, Mary Kay Cosmetics), Presidents Ronald Reagan and John F. Kennedy, Peter Jennings (ABC News) and Stephen Jobs (co-founder, and former President and Chairman of Apple Computer).

They, too, possess the basic qualities needed for success, but with the possible exception of Jobs, none would be considered ultra-intelligent or authoritative. I categorize these successes as charismatic because their major strength comes from an innate propensity to inspire, to lead, and to instill trust in others.

In climbing the corporate career ladder, the brightest stars and fastest climbers are charismatic. Technically, they are capable, but most are less than outstanding; if there's need for technical expertise, they find an expert. "People skill" is the expertise of charismatics. They are gregarious, open-minded, and politically astute; many possess the risk-taking spirit of the entrepreneur. Being strong believers in the "team" concept (although not always good team-players), these employees usually become participatory managers. Charismatics seem and sometimes are genuinely caring of others, but manipulation is their forte and it pays dividends in advancement.

The authoritative person is a commander, but the charismatic is a leader. In the business world, success might be attained through the power and superiority of one's basic skills accompanied by low charisma; progress up the ladder is relatively slow. Charisma or "people skills" alone is insufficient for success; one must possess, at the very least, average intelligence, knowledge and business ability. The ultimate charismatic owns a powerful combination of personality and mental assets. An intelligent "people person" can go fast and far in the corporate structure, if he or she is willing to pay the personal price.

Above all else, ambition is the most important personal quality necessary for success, and it is common to both authoritative and charismatic climbers. Ambition is that hard-driving, competitive psychological force inculcated by American socialization and belief in meritocracy. This inner drive yearns for achievement, yearns to win, yearns to be #1, often at any cost. For many, achievement needs are so strong that the career takes precedence over all other facets of life: personal needs, family, friends, etc. The job simply comes first unless an extreme emergency arises. All the top executives with whom I'm acquainted possess this sacrificial desire for achievement.

. . . . .

Donald E. Petersen
▲▲▲▲▲▲▲▲▲▲▲▲▲▲▲▲▲▲▲▲▲▲▲▲▲▲▲▲▲▲▲▲▲▲

Chairman of the board, Ford Motor Company

It has occurred to me that the question of qualitative observation of successful people is a fairly elusive commodity. There are, however, some special attributes which I believe have redeeming value in helping to support the personal ambitions of aspiring individuals. They are:

Never compromise your personal integrity. Be willing to examine decisions with a set of critical values that remain true to your beliefs.

Enrich those around you; whether they are subordinates or peers, each deserves the benefit of your best thinking and ideas.

Treat people with respect and dignity; trust in fundamental human capability to do the very best possible.

Work as a team player. The game is neither won nor lost by one person, but is rather a composite of the group effort.

. . . . .

Adele M. Scheele
▲▲▲▲▲▲▲▲▲▲▲▲▲▲▲▲▲▲▲▲▲▲▲▲▲▲▲▲▲▲

Labor negotiator; management consultant; author, *Skills For Success* (Ballantine, 1981), *Making College Pay Off* (Ballantine, 1983)

What are the hallmarks of successful people? The research that I've done and the constant interviewing that I do makes me expect that successful people have developed a great deal of personal courage. They also have some understanding of how to relate to the group they work with. The third thing is that they have a notion of their career and moving in it; they have some concept that they're going to try things and are going to become known in their profession.

The first characteristic—developing personal change—involves pushing out the boundaries of what might be a self-definition. You only get to do that by doing things that change or advance your concept of who you are. It's conceptually a way to learn to trust yourself. It comes from an act of doing something or having experienced something. And when you do that on ever-increasing levels, you seem to have more and more courage to try more things.

It can happen early in life, in middle life or late in life. And for the most successful people, it seems to occur fairly constantly, or at least cyclically. So that they might start early, in high school or college, being extremely involved in one person's research, or taking specialized courses they really like.

And they seem to push it. For instance, there was a lawyer in Los Angeles who had never lost a case. He's now a judge. But when I looked at what he did as a high school student, he sold notions in a grocery store, which is not exacly what you'd call high stakes. But what he did was set up experiments for himself, and one of them was to try to tell the buyers from the nonbuyers from the people who would approach his counter. Or he'd try to make everybody who came by his counter make a purchase. Once he could do that, you can understand how every juror would vote for him.

Also under personal courage there's the idea that you can risk your own reputation, that you can risk not appearing too much an idiot, and connect yourself to a new idea, to a new group, new people, or whatever.

It's that risk–linking that I know all successful people do in spades.

The not so successful people are what I call sustainers. They're stuck. They're so afraid they'll screw up and be humiliated that they won't try again.

It's not that people who are successful love having things not work out. It's just that they've learned not to personalize it so much. And they at least learn what not to do again. Whereas the not successful people learn never to try again. That happens all through life.

The second characteristic has to do with how you relate to the organization or group, that is, the core of people you have to work with. Successful people learn two things—one is that you have to be a good team player, and the other is that you have to be an expert contributor, either a star or expert in some part.

You support and care for your team or group. At the same time, the team or group has to see you as someone who is more valuable than merely for the job you do.

Successful people care about their professions. They begin to know some of the people who are as good as or better than they are. They kind of catapult themselves through these people, their ideas and their connections.

Later, when they're beginning to accomplish things, successful people don't mind magnifying what they've done. They might do some public relations. They certainly don't turn the other way when it comes to them.

Unsuccessful people do. However, they don't *say* they're turning aside opportunities. They might say that the award involved is too small. Or a publication asked them to do an article but it was without pay. Or they were asked to speak at a conference but it wasn't big enough. They don't seem to realize that there is growth in these things, that you can start small and work up. They don't seem to realize that they're turning their backs on any light that might shine.

. . . . .

Alan Bean
Astronaut, *Apollo* 12 and *Skylab* 2

The most important quality I have noticed in successful people is *that they have a dream*. They want to be someone or something. They want to have something. They want to go somewhere.

They think and work toward that dream every day.

I often ask people who tell me their dream, "What did you do today to move closer to your dream?" Eighty-five percent didn't do anything. They are planning to do something next week; they're just too busy today. These eighty-five percent will probably never see their dream come true.

Ask yourself the same question—"What have I done today to make my dream come true?" If the answer is nothing specific, then you will never make it unless you change your ways.

. . . . .

William A. Cohen, PhD

Professor of marketing, associate chairman, department of marketing, California State University, Los Angeles; editor; consultant; author, *The Corporate Strategist's Guide to Corporate Planning* (Wiley, 1982), *The Entrepreneur & Small Business Problem Solver; A Complete Guide to Owning & Operating Your Own Business* (Wiley, 1983), *The Executive's Guide to Finding a Superior Job* (American Management Association, 1983), *How to Make It Big as a Consultant* (American Management Association, 1985)

"Cohen's Maxims" is what I call my list of important qualities that successful people have. They include:

RISK. Never be afraid to take risks. If you work for someone, that is part of what you are paid for. If you work for yourself, it is the only way to become successful.

RESPONSIBILITY. If you are assigned a task, you are responsible for its successful completion. There are no acceptable excuses for failing to fulfill this responsibility and the responsibility cannot be shifted to others.

SELF-CONFIDENCE. Self-confidence comes from successfully completing increasingly difficult tasks and assignments. Give your maximum to every project, no matter how insignificant or formidable.

LEADERSHIP. A leader accepts responsibility for others. This means that the welfare of those you lead must always come before your own well-being. Therefore, while your primary duty is the accomplishment of your organization's mission, the welfare of your subordinates comes second and your own welfare last.

SUCCESS. Success does not come from working hard. Success comes from playing hard. Therefore, if you want success, you must position yourself so that the duties that you perform, no matter how difficult or challenging, are considered play to you and not work. If you do this, not only will you gain success, but you will have fun doing it.

INDIVIDUAL ABILITY. Every individual has the potential to do great things. To reach this potential it is necessary to discover your special abilities and qualifications. This means that you should always attempt new tasks and accept responsibility for untried assignments whenever they are offered.

DUTY. Whatever your occupation, you have a duty to the society of which you are a member. If you are a soldier, your duty is to protect that society. If you are in business or industry, your duty is to create and manage the jobs, wealth, and products of that society. Therefore, failure will be harmful not only to you, but also to society, just as success will be beneficial not only to you, but also to society.

PLANNING. Successful actions are not results of accidents or luck, but rather of an analysis of the situation and the preparation and proper execution of plans. Because of a changing environment and other variables, plans will not always succeed as originally conceived. But planning will maximize your successes and minimize your failures.

COMPENSATION. Compensation, whether in the form of profit, salary, or job satisfaction, is the by-product of your contribution. It is an error to make compensation the focus of your life's work. You will not reach your full potential and will have cheated society of the full benefit of your talent and ability.

. . . . .

Barbara Sher
▲▲▲▲▲▲▲▲▲▲▲▲▲▲▲▲▲▲▲

Founder, Women's Success Teams; lecturer, New York University, New School for Social Research; time management consultant and problem-solving consultant, Mt. Sinai Medical School, New York City Board of Education and major corporations; author, Wishcraft, How to Get What You Really Want (Viking, 1979)

My biggest, most profound secret as to what distinguishes a winner from a nonwinner is support. I don't believe it's any inner characteristic at all. Everybody says persistence and positive attitude are what are important. When I hear that I want to ride out on my white horse and break their necks.

I think positive thinking damages you. I think it encourages you to brainwash yourself. I think that when you feel good, you think you finally deserve to go to heaven and that you're going to get what God meant for you. And if you're in a bad mood, you're not only unhappy, but you think you deserve everything crappy that comes your way. You think you are self-destructive, and you think that people who are going to win never have these bad moods. That's such hogwash!

If you have to improve yourself to get somewhere, forget it. I can think in a positive fashion. I can tell myself I'm good. I can turn off those negative feelings. I can make myself feel wonderful for a minute, or for a day or for a week. But then I go back to whatever I was before.

I don't think the people who have gotten somewhere have any more character or any better temperament or are any more positive than anyone else. I think they have rotten moods. They smoke and they're fat, and they probably take drugs, for all I know.

The truth of the matter is that if you stick to something, you'll get there. And if you don't, you won't. That I believe in. But how do you stick with something? Not with an attitude.

I decided early-on in the game, after a few tries, that I had no character at all. I thought I was never going to make it. Whatever it was you had to do, I couldn't do it. I still can't stay on a diet for more than an hour-and-a-half. I can't even remember which diet I'm on. I jogged once; I finally gave the shoes away.

Instead of trying to be a winner, which made me feel rotten, I decided to work backwards—to figure something I had stuck to, something I *had* accomplished in my life.

By the time I had failed at the thousandth fabulous thing I was going to do, I sat down and asked myself, "What have you ever done?" I think I was almost forty at the time (I'm fifty now). One thing I had done was get through college, although it took me longer than anyone else—seven years, because I liked dropping out. I had done some writing—some papers in college. I wrote them on the last day of Christmas vacation like everyone else, but I did write them.

And I had gotten some good grades. I did, by cramming the night before; I never did anything the way you were supposed to do it. But I never knew anyone who did.

So I got through college eventually. And I raised two children all alone (I'm divorced). And I held onto jobs (some of them much longer than I wanted to, because I hated them).

What enabled me to accomplish these things? I asked myself. It sure wasn't a positive attitude. No, I did those things because I *had* to do them. In each case, I saw there was a structure.

When I was by myself and decided to read all the books I had ever wanted to read, but had never gotten around to reading them, or decided to go on a diet, or save money, or name it, I wouldn't do it. But when I was surrounded by some kind of system that required me to do something, then I'd do it. Like when children scream, you feed them. You go to a job, because if you don't you'll get fired. You write the paper, or you get an F. I decided that this was natural and normal for me. But whether it was natural or normal or not, I—who had no character—clearly had to fall back on what had worked in the past, not what ought to work.

Out of this thinking I evolved what I call the Buddy System. Two friends make it a shared goal to meet both of their individual goals. It works because it's a thousand times easier to have faith,

courage and good ideas for someone else than it is for yourself—
and easier for someone else to have them for you.

I did it on a group basis. I got together a group of people, and
told them, "I'm going to make you do what you want, if you'll
make me do what I want." We met once a week and we made one
another do these things. Pretty soon I had dates for seminars and
ads in the paper. People were calling me on the phone and asking
me about it and some were sending me checks. I had to answer the
phone. I had to go to appointments that were on my calendar. I
had to show up at seminars that were planned. The idea acquired
its own machinery. I didn't need the team any more.

That, esentially, has been my secret. I figure out something I
want to do and then I lock myself into it somehow. It's support.
It's getting all the help you can. Say there's a wall in front of you
and you want to get on the other side of it. The way to do it is to
sit around with a group of people and discuss it, and they'll come
up with ninety-five ways for you to get over that wall. You'll
squawk and whine and complain and say their ideas will never
work. And then you'll go over the wall using one of their ways.

If I wanted to learn math, I'd get together five math-damaged
people like myself, and keep a chapter ahead of them in a textbook.
I'd do that in any subject in which I felt I was ignorant.

I think everybody ought to get a buddy or a team for anything
they want to do, and meet every week. Tell what they did last
week, tell what they had trouble with and tell what they're going
to do next week. I think you could go to the moon that way.

The seminar idea went on to become the book, and my whole
life turned around. I wound up going on every radio and television
show in the country and living on airplanes.

I'm a one-trick pony. I came up with a helluva good idea. And
I haven't changed it much from the day I came up with it. Not
much at all. I'm able to make those seminars work so well, that
anyone who ever has gone through one loves it. I get nothing but
praise and people pay me a lot of money to do it.

I feel gratified because I've been able to stop people from having
to go through the terrible isolation and lack of support that I suffered. I guess I'm like the doctor who hates illness and feels like

he's making a dent in it. My dream is that everybody can put together their own support system so they can quit being discouraged. I want people to ge support and respect—and become themselves. That's what happened to me.

· · · · ·

James B. Irwin

President, High Flight Foundation

I think the most important ingredient to professional success is being single-minded or highly motivated in a specific direction. In other words, you must know where you want to go.

· · · · ·

Patricia O'Toole

Contributing editor, *Manhattan, Inc.*; author, *Corporate Messiah; The Hiring and Firing of Million-Dollar Managers* (Morrow, 1984)

When I was doing my research on *Corporate Messiah,* one of the most interesting people I interviewed was Sanford G. Sigoloff, the 51-year-old Los Angeles executive who specializes in corporate turnarounds; he's a rescue expert. In the early 1970s, Sigoloff turned around Republic Corporation of Los Angeles, a discount retailer and manufacturer of health-care products. A few years later, he successfully maneuvered Daylin Corporation, another failing Southern California retailer, through a bankruptcy. When I met him, he was involved in attempting to save the Wickes Companies, another retailing company but whose main business had once been in lumber and building supplies. With its $4 billion in annual revenues, Wickes was one of the largest U.S. corporations ever to go bankrupt.

"Succeeding takes two things," Sigoloff told me, "the will to win and even more important, the will to prepare." In the situation at Wickes, Sigoloff had to deal with fifteen-thousand creditors that hadn't been paid, thousands of employees, many of whom were going to be fired, and hundreds of stores all over the country. Just to get all of that onto a computer and into some sort of manageable shape, so he could know what the pieces were and figure out how to deal with them, took an incredible amount of just sitting there and doing it—the will to prepare.

I've thought of that many times because there are situations that we all get into where things go wrong because we haven't had the will to prepare. We start acting before we've done our homework.

When Sigoloff takes over a company, he insists that he be granted powers befitting a czar. "My conditions for taking on a turnaround are always the same," he said. "There's only one chief executive officer—me—and he holds all terminal decision-making authority, including authority over the board."

But success, Sigoloff said, "ultimately depends on how much authority you can give up." He believed that a really good executive was one who made the fewest possible decisions. "The only ones a good CEO makes," he said, "are the really unpopular ones that nobody else wants to make, like the ultimate decision to close a plant."

. . . . .

John Torquato
▶▶▶▶▶▶▶▶▶▶▶▶▶▶▶▶▶▶▶▶

Author, *Why Winners Win* (American Management Association, 1983)

Success people are DOERS. They do things.

Most other people are WAITERS and WATCHERS.

WAITERS wait until someone else does something. When it appears safe enough, they jump on the bandwagon.

WATCHERS simply find a safe niche and literally watch the world go by.

DOERS make things happen. They are the shakers and the movers of the world. My message is that everybody could be a doer except for the suffocating fear of risk and failure. DOERS want to win. WAITERS and WATCHERS need to denigrate others to make themselves look good by comparison.

WAITERS and WATCHERS take losses personally. DOERS accept loss as an inevitable part of risk and do not consider it a reflection of their own self-worth.

To those people able to overcome the fear of risk, rejection and failure, true success will manifest itself.

In summary, it is our attitude toward ourselves that dictates what we will be. It has been my experience that most people are self-fulfilling prophecies who lament their lot in life. Yet fate did not make them what they are, their attitude did, and fear of failure solidified the mold.

. . . . .

William A. Anders

Astronaut, *Appolo* 8; senior executive vice president, operations, Textron Inc.

Know your people and trust them, but not so much that you shouldn't have a good and timely set of financial measurements to screen their results by. Even good guys make mistakes.

Delegate authority to match responsibility. Don't expect a home run from a subordinate if you don't let him swing with enough bat. And remember, you can't delegate (avoid) those things your boss holds you responsible for.

Don't fall in love with your product. The shareholders generally don't care what you're selling so long as it's making money. Lack of objectivity generally results in sticking with a dog too long.

2

Becoming More Effective and Efficient

~~~~~~

At the end of the usual working day, are you often frustrated for having failed to accomplish the more important tasks you set for yourself?

Do you sometimes procrastinate so long on work assignments that you end up toiling overtime on weekends to complete them?

Are there papers on your desk, other than reference materials, that you haven't touched for a week or more?

If you answered yes to any of these questions, it's not very likely that you have effective control over your work day. You're probably often the victim of anxiety and stress. You're not working smart.

You're likely to be caught up in what has been called the "activity trap." You sweat at your desk from early morning until early evening, until the office is virtually empty. You keep cutting back on your lunch hour and find yourself lugging home more and more work at night. You're so engulfed in the minute-to-minute frenzy of the work day that you've lost sight of exactly why you are so frenzied; all of that activity has become an end in itself.

If you're at this stage, or approaching it, you have to first understand that time isn't a matter of minutes and hours. It's what you choose to do with time that counts, and the amount of effort you spend doing it. As Thoreau put it, "It's not enough to be busy . . . The question is, what are we busy about?"

It's a matter of being both effective and efficient. Being effective means doing the right job. It means taking the time out to establish goals for yourself and then determine the steps necessary to achieve those goals.

Being efficient has to do with doing the right job right. It assumes you've set goals and the means for accomplishing them. Efficiency involves performance and productivity.

The more upwardly mobile you are, the greater your need for effectiveness and efficiency. Once you've become outstandingly successful in your profession or achieved the topmost rung of the ladder at the firm where you're employed, effectiveness and efficiency are not quite so important. You have assistants and secretaries to keep things running smoothly for you. But to the average man or woman on the white-collar fast track, avoiding confusion and chaos is more of a head-to-head struggle.

AUDITING YOUR TIME

How do you spend your average working day? You should be able to answer that question in very specific terms before attempting to establish your goals and priorities. To most people who look back on their day, the hours are merely a blur. Most of what they did, they did out of habit or a sense of urgency. They have little real understanding of how their time was spent hour by hour, task by task.

A time audit will help you to come to a realization of how you are using your most valuable resource. Essentially, a time audit means keeping careful track of what you do, when, on several "typical" days. It brings your work patterns into sharp focus and helps you make the distinction between achievement and mere activity. It is an important tool in learning to work smart.

If you're like most people who complete the audit, you're likely to be surprised at what it reveals—the amount of time you misuse during the day and the different ways you have for misusing it. Once you've completed the audit and begin to analyze it, pinpointing the time-wasting activities, you can begin working toward reducing and eliminating the timewasters.

Plan to audit your time for a period of at least one week. Begin by compiling a list of all your job-related activities. The list will probably include some or most of these items:

1.   Reading (time spent with incoming mail, reports, memos, trade journals, etc.)
2.   Writing (time spent on correspondence, reports, memos, etc.)
3.   Meetings
4.   Telephone time
5.   Travel time (both commuting and business travel)
6.   Planning
7.   Evaluating
8.   Interruptions
9.   Free time (work breaks, lunch breaks)

These are only suggestions. Your own activity list is likely to include several of these plus other items that are specific to your job.

Enter the activity list along the top of the time-audit sheet. Enter the hours you work at one side of the sheet; use half-hour intervals.

Supply yourself with a sheet for each day of the week. It should look like the chart on page 52.

As your day progresses, enter check marks or Xs in the appropriate boxes. Carry the sheet with you at all times. Enter the checks as you're working. If you try to make the entries at the end of the day by relying on your memory, you'll find it's difficult to be exact.

If you're involved in a wide variety of activities and move frequently from one to another, a time audit based on half-hour intervals may not give you an accurate enough picture of your day. If this happens to be true, draw up a sheet using 15-minute intervals.

No matter the interval length, make the audit sheet as detailed as you can. If you're interrupted during a planning session by a drop-in visitor, make a note of how long the interruption lasts. If you're kept on "hold" before beginning a telephone conversation, write down the length of the delay. Keep track of how much time you spend daydreaming. All such time should be charted just as carefully—even *more* carefully—than productive time.

ANALYZING THE AUDIT

Once you've completed the audit, add up the time in each category. When you have the totals, a number of questions can be asked, as:

What activities are taking most of your time? On which ones are you spending the least time?

Compare the time being spent on such categories as Meetings and Planning with the results being achieved. What activities are

	Reading	Writing	Meetings	Telephone time	Travel time	Planning	Evaluation	Interruptions	Free time			
8:00												
8:30												
9:00												
9:30												
10:00												
10:30												
11:00												
11:30												
NOON												
12:30												
1:00												
1:30												
2:00												
2:30												
3:00												
3:30												
4:00												
4:30												
5:00												
5:30												
6:00												
6:30												
7:00												
7:30												
8:00												

producing the most results? What activities are producing the least? Are you surprised at how much time you spend on the phone? Can you combine bits of telephone time into a telephone period during which you take care of all or most of your calls?

What activities deserve increased effort? What activities can be cut back?

Are there some activities that can be eliminated? Are there some that can be delegated?

How much of your time is being chewed up by interruptions? How many times a day do interruptions arise? Can you control them?

And analyze your day-to-day activities in relation to your goals. Are these activities contributing to the attainment of your goals? If the answer is no in certain categories, perhaps you should consider eliminating them. Add other activities that will help you achieve your goals.

In general, the audit should provide you with information to help make your day more productive. It's a good idea to take a time audit at regular intervals, every six months, say. It will be less revealing each time you do it, but it can still be helpful in encouraging efficiency.

SETTING GOALS

If you want to make effective use of your workday, you need to get into the habit of focusing your attention on the most important task of the moment. That task is not necessarily the one that looms as the most urgent, nor is it likely to be the task that arrives with the next telephone call or is presented by the individual who comes walking through your open office door.

To determine what's important *now*, you first have to establish individual goals for yourself and work out detailed plans for achieving them. Every book and every seminar on the subject of time management stresses the need for goal-setting and planning. And most men and women who have reached a management level agree that both are vitally important. Yet many of these same managers fail to plan. The reason? Planning takes time, and they simply don't have any time. Don't get caught up in this paradox.

Setting goals is hardly a secret.

Make your goals as specific as you can. Put them in writing. This will help to make them clearer. It also will deepen the commitment you have to each one.

The goals you set for yourself are likely to fall into several different categories. These include:

Career. Reach a certain professional level; get promoted to a higher position; be given greater responsibility; learn a new job skill; complete a certain project in a specific amount of time.

Financial. Earn a certain amount of money within a specified time; get advanced to a higher salary level; set up an investment program tailored to your income.

Educational. Earn credits toward a degree; take courses in subjects in which you've always been interested.

Physical Fitness. Jog three or four times a week; join a health club; diet; quit smoking.

Community/Charitable. Do volunteer work at a local hospital at least once a week; sign up with Literacy Volunteers or a similar organization.

Personal. Work to become less anxious, hostile, jealous or insecure; meet new people; cultivate new friendships.

Leisure. Do something really different: Go dragboat racing or whale watching; visit a city or country you've never been to before; join an archaeological dig in Mexico; raise cocker spaniels.

Once you've identified your most important goals, the next step is to map out plans to achieve each one. Give these plans a priority among all other items that demand your attention.

SETTING PRIORITIES

Tom Landry of the Dallas Cowboys, one of the most successful coaches in pro football history, get things done by following a piece of advice he heard many years ago. The advice was derived from an anecdote about a salesman by the name of Irving Levy who called on the president of Bethlehem Steel during the Depression and told him that he had an idea that would enable him to become more successful. The president told Levy that he wasn't interested in becoming more successful, but he was interested in any idea that would enable him to get more things done each day.

Levy told him that he had an idea that would allow him to do more than he had ever done before if he would just try it for 30 days. The president agreed and Levy told him to take out a piece of paper and list all of the things that he had to do the next day. Once he had finished the list, Levy told him that he should now put the things to do in the order of importance from "one" to the end of his list. And after he had done that, Levy told him to put it in his pocket and when he arrived at his office the next day to start on the first item of his list and then to attend to each item until he had finished his list. If he didn't finish it, Levy told him not to worry because he had been working on the most important things that he had to do.

Levy then told the president that he could pay him anything he thought the idea was worth. After 30 days, the president called Levy back and had him come into his office where he gave Levy a check for $25,000, an impressive sum of money during the Depression. He told Levy that this was the best idea that he had received.

Says Landry: "I have used this same idea for many years and have found that I can accomplish more things with this method than from any other idea I have ever received."

Alan Lakein, a leading expert on personal time management, offered suggestions on setting priorities in a detailed agenda in his landmark book, *How to Get Control of Your Time and Your Life*. He recommended ranking both job goals and personal goals according to an A, B, C system:

A—A goal of high value and major importance; must be done.
B—A goal of low, lesser importance; should be done.
C—A goal of low value; would be nice to do.

The idea, of course, is to begin with the A goals, and when they're accomplished proceed to the Bs and then the Cs.

Make a daily list of activities that will contribute toward the achievement of each goal. Each "To Do" list is a basic tool in the effective and efficient use of your time. Don't leave home without it.

Remember, each "To Do" list must be more than a mere catalog of activities you intend to perform. The activities should be arranged according to their importance; they should be prioritized. Number them from 1 to whatever. Thus you will begin each day doing the activity coded A-1, then proceed to A-2, A-3 and downwards. Once you've completed all of the A tasks, you move on to those labeled B-1, B-2 and so on, and, if there is time remaining in the day, to the Cs.

When it comes to arranging your daily schedule, block out chunks of time to handle the most important projects. Be sure to leave some breathing space in your schedule. A tight schedule often produces stress. For example, if you feel that a scheduled meeting is going to last about an hour, allot an hour-and-a-quarter for it on your daily schedule.

Since it is impossible to predict what is going to happen during an average work day, be prepared to reorder your priorities based upon what transpires. Consult your "To Do" list every hour or so and consider whether an updating is necessary.

At day's end, give the list a final check. Maybe you've been able to accomplish every item on the A list and even a few Bs. That's great. But even if you've only been able to accomplish one or two A items, take heart in the fact that you've spent your time working on activities of the highest importance. That, in itself, should give you a feeling of satisfaction.

A final word. Realize that you cannot control everything. You can't complete the report the boss wants if the photocopier breaks down. You can't get to the airport on time if you happen to encounter a monstrous traffic jam. Once in a while, you're going to meet up with such calamities. Try to take them in stride instead of feeling you've been thwarted.

DIVIDE AND CONQUER

When you look over your list of goals, you'll instantly realize that these goals present you with much more to do than it's possible to accomplish at any one time. The solution is to divide each goal into manageable parts. In other words, list all of the activities necessary toward achieving each goal. For example, if your goal is writing a report, the first step is to make sure you have the right paraphernalia—pens, pencils, paper—and the necessary research materials before you begin so you won't be distracted by having to look for them. If you have a personal goal of learning to speak French, your first goal may be to call the admissions offices of local schools or colleges to find out what courses are available.

Establishing short-term, easily attainable goals has more than a merely practical value. It has an emotional aspect as well. When you divide long-term goals into a series of sub-goals, and then begin achieving the sub-goals, each achievement bolsters your confidence and encourages you to do more. Without sub-goals, you're not likely to see much progress, and it's easy to become discouraged.

DECISION-MAKING

Becoming more effective and efficient also means sharpening your skills as a decision-maker. The higher up the ladder you climb, the more important the decisions you'll be called upon to make and the greater the impact they're likely to have.

In making a decision, begin by clarifying your objectives. What do you want the decision to accomplish? You should be able to state the answer to that question simply and clearly.

Decisions are based on data. Get the facts you need. Read whatever relevant material is available on the subject. Talk to knowledgeable people.

Try to develop at least three alternatives. Compare each alternative with your objective. Pick the alternative that comes closest to achieving what you want to achieve.

Once the decision has been made and acted upon, evaluate it. Did your decision lead to the achievement of the goal? If it didn't, try to determine why it didn't. Maybe the goal wasn't stated clearly enough. Maybe you didn't perceive all of the alternatives. Maybe your timing was poor. A premature decision, for example, is likely to be regarded as an unnecessary decision.

Don't make a decision when there's no need to do so. A decision is often disruptive. Someone or some group is likely to be displeased by it. When you make an unnecessary decision, you're likely to be regarded more as a meddler than a manager.

Learn to distinguish between those decisions you can reverse and those you can't. The decision to hold the annual sales conference in Atlantic City is reversible, at least for a time. The decision to fire someone isn't.

A reversible decision can always be nullified, and other plans substituted. In the case of an irreversible decision, you're committed forever. Most decisions are neither totally reversible or irreversible. They fall between the two poles.

When it comes to making a reversible decision, there's no reason not to move fast. If it fails to produce the desired results, you can always backtrack. Irreversible decisions should be pondered carefully.

Some people are inclined to make decisions based on hunches. They believe their solution is right but they're unable to cite the reasons. "I have a gut feeling about this," is the way they explain it.

There are good hunches and bad hunches. The latter are sometimes triggered by a desire to accept the first solution that becomes obvious. Bad hunches are sometimes the result of an emotional or a prejudicial reaction to a situation.

Good hunches, on the other hand, are based on intuitive thinking. We perceive the solution without logical reasoning, processing the data in our subconscious. This is a normal process. Excellent decisions are often based on hunches of this type.

Even if your hunches are usually good, don't try to justify a hunch based decision at a board meeting. Unless you own the company, it's usually best to rely on the analytical and linear approach to decision-making.

. . . . .

Additional Reading

Management; Tasks, Responsibilities, Practices, by Peter F. Drucker (Harper, 1985; first published 1979). An explanation of the knowledge and skills important in the art; a management classic.

The Effective Executive, by Peter F. Drucker (Harper, 1985; first published 1967). An examination of the five practices essential to business effectiveness—managing time, choosing what to contribute, mobilizing strength, setting priorities and decision-making.

Managing for Results, by Peter F. Drucker (Harper, 1986; first published 1964). Opportunities that make the organization prosper and grow.

Managing, by Harold Geneen (Avon, 1984). Secrets for corporate success from the former CEO at ITT.

Up the Ladder; Coping With the Corporate Climb, by Thomas Friedman (Warner, 1986). Case studies of corporate managers.

No-Nonsense Management, by Robert S. Sloma (Bantam, 1981). Seventy guiding principles to help you learn to think as top management does.

The Iacocca Management Technique, by Maynard F. Gordon (Dodd, Mead, 1985). How Iacocca did it; illuminating reading.

EXPERT ADVICE

Being effective means indentifying your goal, the course of action you plan to pursue. Efficiency has to do with how you attain that

goal. By combining the two, concentrating on being effective first
and then worrying about being efficient, you get results. Naturally
everyone applies this lesson in a highly personal way. As the expert
advice below indicates, what works for one person impedes work
for another.

"For me, lists kill," says writer Whitley Strieber. "When I
write . . . it's a total adventure. I don't know what's going to
happen next." Whereas popular psychologist and author Dr. Joyce
Brothers makes a mental list each night before bed of the three
most important things she hopes to accomplish the following day.
Chemistry professor Hans E. Suess thrives in a kind of controlled
chaos; he works by brainstorms not by prioritized schedules. Mel-
vin R. Goodes, president of Warner-Lambert, advises careful and
clear organization, including working against project lists, under-
taking key projects during prime time and maintaining a system
for following up. Theatrical producer Alexander Cohen stays on
top of his hectic work load by making Saturday one of his most
productive days.

To increase your own effectiveness and efficiency, you must
devise a work strategy that suits your particular needs. As you read
through the following pages, try to keep in mind how you can
apply the advice of the experts to your own situation.

. . . . .

Alexander Cohen

Theatrical and television producer

I'm a workaholic, and the consequence is that I don't think I'm a
very good subject for your book; I don't have any "smarts."

I get up very early in the morning—about 6:30—and I'm at
work at eight o'clock, usually with a breakfast date. I'm in the
office at about nine, and I generally follow a routine. I work until
about five minutes of one, when I go dashing off to some lunch
meeting that I've set up. Since I work as a theatrical and television

producer, I'm involved with a great number of personalities and advertising agencies who, in turn, have another layer of personalities, so I use virtually every lunch to either continue or cultivate relationships. My day usually ends by my leaving this office at about five minutes of eight and going to the theatre—somewhere. If it's Off Broadway and very far downtown, like Circle in the Square or Cherry Lane, then obviously I have to leave at 7:30 or 7:40. On nights that I don't do that, I'm generally in the office until nineish or 9:30. And then I go to dinner.

While we—my wife and partner Hildy Parks and I—have many friends, we also have a very large circle of acquaintances. So a lot of evenings are spent essentially enjoying ourselves, but still cultivating these relationships. I find in this business that your paths keep crossing.

We're always here on Saturday. That's a house rule. It's limited to the degree that I'm not with a full staff, but with my assistant, Gail Rosenblum, Laurie on the switchboard, and one or two messengers and the car. But they can be backed up. We find that Saturdays are very productive days because the volume of telephone calls is cut to virtually nothing. So we use our Saturdays—and I've been doing that since 1942.

Sunday is reading. But at least that can be done propped up in bed. It's reading all the things that have accumulated here during the course of a week and for one reason or another have to be read by me. Mostly it's the plays that are considered productive by those who read for this office. And I'll read some reports from the Actors Fund of America, which is very close to me, very close to my heart.

I also spend my Sundays watching the morning programming of the networks, which is the only programming I commend. I must say I also watch "Nightline." I think the news departments of the networks do some pretty interesting stuff.

. . . . .

Dr. Joyce Brothers
~~~~~~~~~~~~~~~~~~~~~~~~~~~~~~~~~~~

Psychologist; columnist; author, *What Every Woman Ought to Know About Love and Marriage* (Simon & Schuster, 1984), *What Every Woman Ought to Know About Men* (Ballantine, 1985)

Before I go to sleep at night, I make a mental note of the three most important things that I must do the next day, ranking them in order of importance. The next day I start by making a stab at accomplishing each one. Once I've done these things—or at least made an attempt to do each—I feel that I'm free to do whatever I want to do with the day. I've found that if I don't follow this policy, I tend to procrastinate or do unimportant things first, and I may never get to the important things at all.

. . . . .

John Devaney
~~~~~~~~~~~~~~~~~~~~~~~~~~~~~~~

Editor; author, *Great Sports Stars of Yesteryear*; *Where Are They Today* (Crown, 1985) *Winners of the Heisman Trophy* (Walker, 1986), *Lyndon Johnson, President* (Walker, 1986)

For many years I thought I could never write a book—50,000 to 100,000 words seeming an impossible task to someone accustomed to writing no more than 3,000 to 4,000 words for a magazine article. Gradually, under the gun of a signed contract to do my first book, I convinced myself that a book is only 15 to 30 magazine articles, and that if I could write an article in a week, I could write a book in six months.

As a magazine writer, I would set goals for myself, usually 10 manuscript pages per day. I set the same goal for myself in writing a book. I marked down ten Xs on a sheet of paper each morning. I checked each X off with a red marker as I finished each page. If I failed to do the 10, I circled in green the Xs undone. The next day

I tried to catch up. I marked the green circles with red checks as I did the undone pages of the day before, then tried to check off ten more Xs in red. Those red Xs were visible, easy-to-see proof of my progress toward a goal. It was a goal so far away—the first 300-page draft of a book—that I couldn't visualize it. If I had tried, I might have panicked and been unable to reach it. But ten Xs, circled in red, were goals I could see passed, and that passage in six to eight hours left me feeling both satisfied and confident. By accomplishing each day's goal (even each hour's goal because sometimes I broke down the work into so many pages per hour), I could sense I was taking measurable steps toward a faraway goal.

I'm a fantastic list person. In the evening, I make a list of what I want to accomplish the next day—so many pages of copy to be turned out, so many magazines to be read, persons I want to phone, persons to see and to write to. I usually write in the morning, research (read, do library work or interview) in the early afternoon, and devote the late afternoon and evening to personal and family responsibilities. I fit my list into each of these categories.

As I begin the day, I make another list, an hour-by-hour list of goals for the morning's writing. I write down Xs on a sheet of paper to indicate how many pages of copy I hope to turn out. As I finish a page, I check an X in red. After a certain number of checked-off Xs, I give myself a break for a stroll around the block or a can of Coke—a reward for reaching a particular goal.

I also make a list of phone calls I want to complete. I check in red the names of people I'm able to reach. I circle in green those I don't reach.

When I write letters, I use the same system—a red check when a letter gets mailed, a green circle meaning it will be done later, probably the next day.

. . . . .

Whitley Strieber

Author, *The Wolfen* (Bantam, 1979), *Black Magic* (Morrow, 1982), *The Night Church* (Simon & Schuster, 1983), *Warday* (with James Kunetka, Warner, 1985), *Nature's End* (with James Kunetka, 1986)

For me, lists kill. When I write, I have to feel as if I'm in front of a blank screen. It's a total adventure. I don't know what's going to happen next.

When I go to bed at night, I never know what I'm going to be writing the next morning. I always have to be surprised.

I usually get up around 7:00 a.m. I take a walk after sending my son off to school and usually begin work around 9:00 a.m.

I try to work very steadily during the day. At about 10:30, I usually have a cup of tea. Around noon, I have a light lunch. Then I work through until around six or so. In the evenings, I really don't "turn off." I go into another kind of mode where I'll read things that relate to what I'm writing. The same thing is true on weekends.

I do relax occasionally. Mostly I work. Or I'm with my family, my son and my wife.

During the course of a day—especially in the early afternoon—I fall into a sort of state that I consider to be very important for my work. I get to feel very heavy, but not tired exactly. I'll lie down and there will proceed a lot of very vivid thoughts relating to what I'm writing.

These thoughts consist of a sort of a symbolized representation of what I'm working on. When I was writing *Warday,* these symbols—or schematics, you could call them—represented the total military relationship between the United States and the Soviet Union, and the way in which a particular military manisfestation, the strategic defense system, would cause the relationship to go out of balance.

That's how my ideas work. They don't work in terms of thoughts. They work in terms of symbol groups—schematics.

Sometimes there will be visual imagery as well. I might see the face of a character that I'm working on in a book, and the image will be very important to the story. In other words, the expression might imply what I'm going to write about for the rest of the day. But mostly it's the symbolic material that's important.

On a deep level, I feel there is an organization, there is a definite structure. But when you look at it, it changes. It isn't something that can be pinned down.

I could no more write you a list of my life's plan than the man in the moon. I have no idea what it might be. If I wrote the list, something would be diminished. I would have less of a life. Just as if I planned out a novel, it would be less of a book.

· · · · ·

Leonard Maltin

Movie critic, "Entertainment Tonight" (Off-network television show)

I have only one "secret" and it's not very original: I'm a list-maker. I find that the only way I get things done is to make daily lists— often scribbled on the backs of envelopes—and cross out the entries as I do them. What's funny about this system is that I find almost as much satisfaction in the actual elimination of items from my lists as I do in the completion of the jobs themselves! Whatever psychological benefit that may provide, it does seem to help me accomplish a fair amount.

I also find that getting a lot of little chores done the first thing in the morning sets me up for the whole day. Knowing that by 10 or 11 a.m. I've already managed to make some calls, dash off a couple of notes, or run an errand or two lets me take a deep breath, and move on to more serious projects. Otherwise I might have those chores nagging at me all day long, and interrupting the time (and concentration) I need to do what's really important.

. . . . .

Robert H. Breckinridge

President, Vitronics Corporation

The most important factor of management, and I would include time management in that area, is to surround yourself with good people. Of particular importance is to get someone who can replace you. Unfortunately, there seems to be a fear of doing this on the part of many people. My thinking is that the only way you can get promoted is to make sure that there's a person who can take your job.

. . . . .

Robert Alwine

Group vice president, Engineered Products-Worldwide (Uniroyal, Inc.)

As my "secrets" for managing time successfully, I offer the following:

> Always keep key objectives in mind.
> Sort complexity to concentrate on the right actions.
> Develop methods and a network to have others work as activists for you in an orderly way.
> Step lively and step up to issues and impediments.
> Maintain the discipline of a daily "to do and follow" list.
> Say thank you and show you care, for working Smart means getting positive results, and doing so over and over again depends on people and their attitudes and enthusiasm.

. . . . .

Melvin R. Goodes

President and chief operating officer, Warner-Lambert Company

The following are methods that I have used to increase the productivity of my time:

> Set up a block of time where one will not be interrupted.
> Ensure that key projects are undertaken during prime working time.
> Always work against project lists of relative importance.
> Make liberal use of a color coding system in determining response to correspondence.
> Maintain an extensive follow-up system.

Once these become a part of one's daily work habits, productivity is bound to increase.

. . . . .

Kathy Keeton

President, *Omni* magazine; author, *Woman of Tomorrow* (St. Martin's, 1985)

I think that the best technique I have employed over the years in business for managing my time is adherence to a rule to make quick decisions on small matters. In addition, I hire good staff and leave them alone provided they meet assigned objectives. I have also learned to rely more and more on the computer to manage my time. I use it for everything from routine scheduling to important research. For example, I may not be an expert, but before I go off to lunch with a Nobel prize-winning DNA scientist I turn to my personal computer and retrieve my file on molecular biology.

. . . . .

Vern O. Curtis

President, Denny's, Inc.

Here's what successful people do:

Frequently evaluate the use of their time.
Have long and short term goals.
Plan time use weekly or daily if necessary.
Develop a priority reminder system.
Drop low priority time wasters whenever possible.
Delegate.
Keep notes as to high-priority things to do.
Handle paperwork once.
Know what they can and cannot control.
Have a "do it now" approach.
Block out consistent time periods to accomplish certain things.
Keep trying.

. . . . .

Rev. Theodore M. Hesburgh
President, University of Notre Dame

I find the best way to save time is to have more to do than I can possibly get done in the time available. Then I seem to manage to get twice as much done. I get the least done when I have time on my hands.

Obviously, the other best way to use time well is not to waste it. This means knowing exactly what has to get done and getting at it, preferably under some pressure. This, of course, is only the other side of the above coin.

. . . . .

Don M. Berry
Chairman, StarTel

I start companies; StarTel was my tenth, and I have started several since then, so I am sometimes very busy. I have two unique methods of coping with my time demands:

Go to work Sunday night at 9:00 p.m. and don't return home until: (a) All correspondence, memo(s) or documentation is current or; (b) You have only time to shower and return to work. Either (a) or (b) results in being prepared for Monday, the start of a new week.

Sleep on plane trips. I travel a lot and since I can easily sleep on the plane, I will often work through the night, get on the plane in the morning and sleep as I travel.

. . . . .

Bob G. Alexander
President, Alexander Energy Corporation

I think one of our "key secrets" is our staff meetings we have on every Monday. We have lunch brought in to our conference room, and from 11:30 a.m. to 1:30 p.m. we talk about accomplishments from last week and what we are going to do the following week. Here we can iron out any departmental problems or communication problems and assess how well we solved the previous problems. I find this to be an important two hours, and it only takes the department heads away from their areas for one hour. They would have to eat lunch away from their areas if they were not in the meeting.

. . . . .

Hans E. Suess
Professor of chemistry, University of California, San Diego

I have a most unorthodox way of doing my work. I don't keep things in shape. In my opinion, people spend much too much time keeping things tidy and nice to look at. If I were to do that, I'd spend all of my time keeping things in one drawer, and other things in other drawers. And once in a while when I'm looking for something, I'll take things out and try to get them in order. But not before.

I don't set priorities. I know what I have to get done, and I try to stick to that, and do one thing after another.

Efficiency in my case doesn't depend on how I organize my time. It's a question of having sort of a brainstorm. If I have an idea—and I can get fascinated by my ideas—I work on it.

I don't really follow a schedule during the day. But one develops.

I'm very disorganized, people say. But I get things done. When the time comes, I do things.

I'm retired now. But I can't stop working. Actually, I'm getting more done now than at the time when I was obligated to do things. Then I had to stick to a certain schedule. And there were more deadlines than I wanted. I hate deadlines. When I had many urgent things to do, I never knew which ones to do first, and I never got anything done.

I don't make lists. I don't set priorities. I want to be able to do things when I feel like doing them.

My wife is very unhappy about the way I do things. She thinks I should do what she wants me to do. Help her, and so on. When I feel like helping her, I help her.

I never try to be in a hurry.

. . . . .

Bonnie McCullough

Lecturer; columnist; author, *Totally Organized* (St. Martin's, 1986; with Bev Cooper, *76 Ways to Be Organized for Christmas* (St. Martin's, 1982), *Bonnie's Household Organizer* (St. Martin's, 1980)

Naturally organized people have an inborn instinct that helps them arrange things in orderly fashion. If something is out of line, they are uneasy until they have taken care of it. They have an urgency to "finish" things. If there is a lot to do, they somehow know what ought to be done first. The unorganized person does not get visual clues or prioritize things in his or her head; they get overwhelmed and quit. It doesn't so much matter that there are two styles of thinking, except that there are some advantages to being at least a little bit organized. You can save time, money and worry and still leave a little fun in your life.

The unorganized person can learn to be more organized. They can retrain themselves, one step at a time. It's like laying down a sprinkling system for your yard. Installation takes time and money, but once it's been installed all you have to do is turn a dial. With things under control, you can charge into new territory.

· · · · ·

Cheryl Waixel

Editor, World: The Magazine for Decision Makers

I list all high-priority deadlines, tasks and phone calls on my calendar the evening before. Then I make sure that all of them are checked off by 5 p.m.—or, in the worst case (when, for example, I've tried but have been unable to reach somebody by phone all day), reprioritized for the next day.

I dispose of 90 percent of my mail as soon as it comes across my desk. Since we have a large communications staff, much of my mail (for example, change-of-address requests from subscribers) can be delegated to somebody else for processing.

I take notes on most of my conversations—phone calls, instructions from my superiors, decisions made at meetings—so that I don't have to ask anybody to repeat information and waste my time and their time in the process.

When I'm impossibly busy—usually around copy deadline time —I don't permit myself to become overwhelmed. I do one thing at a time in order of priority and try to block all distractions out.

I use the phone and avoid personal meetings as much as possible. They take much more time.

Finally, I'm FLEXIBLE. If something isn't working one way, I don't sit around scratching my head forever. I think of another method that may actually succeed.

. . . . .

Terry Davidson

Co-founder, Procrastinators Anonymous

Something that's worked for me but that runs somewhat counter to what time-management specialists advise, has to do with list making. You know what the experts say: make a list of all the things you have to do in the course of a day, then assign priorities to each of the items on the list. Then do the tasks one-by-one in order of importance. I've got nothing against this method, but I think for procrastinators what I call a "countdown list" is better. It can be applied to almost anything that has to be done within a certain amount of time. Let's say you're going to be giving a party, and you've got two weeks in which to get the house ready. Get a sheet of lined paper and make a vertical list of all the days until the party. Instead of filling in each line with the things that you intend to do, leave each line blank. You *know* what has to be done. I don't feel there's any need to make a list. But when you accomplish something, write it down next to the date on which you accomplished it. Pretty soon you'll have a list of all the things you've done. This boosts your confidence and you'll feel like doing even more.

3

Beating the Clock

For those who are seeking to cram as much as possible into each day, Morton Rachofsky, a Dallas realtor, believes he has the answer. He has invented a 25-hour clock. Rachofsky hired a mechanical engineer to put together a timepiece that speeds through the standard hour in 57.6 minutes. Over the 24-hour day, the "found" time—2.4 minutes each hour—adds up to an extra 57.6 minute "hour," which makes for a 25-hour day.

Rachofsky calls his invention XTRAOUR. After getting a patent, Rachofsky made plans to sell the clock nationally for under
$50.

Those who tried scheduling their days on the basis of
XTRAOUR's 25-hour cycle never missed a plane or train or were
late for an appointment. In fact, they showed up anywhere from a
few minutes to an hour early for everything.

Rachofsky insisted that that was no more than a "minor incon-
venience." It was far outweighed, he said, by the advantage of
making the most efficient use of one's time. "There'll always be a
group of achievers who want to squeeze as much as they can into
each day," Rachofsky told *People* magazine. "They'll use it to
speed themselves up a little bit."

Rachofsky's 25-hour clock may be the solution for some people. But there are more practical answers to the riddle of time
management.

First of all, it's important to realize that your work day is made
up of two kinds of time. Most of the day involves time over which
you have little or no control. You are engaged in tasks that are
imposed upon you by the nature of your job or are delegated from
above. Time management specialists call this required time, fixed
time or response time.

Then there is the time you can control, called disposable time
or discretionary time.

If you're like the great majority of people on a management
level, most of your time is fixed time. Indeed, anywhere from 50
to 75 percent of your day is likely to be spent responding to events
and to requests from people. Time management guru Peter
Drucker once noted that no manager ever has more than 25 percent
of his time under control.

While fixed time is obviously important, most time-management experts agree that the key to being an effective manager is
how well you use your discretionary time. What tasks do you
choose to do? How efficiently do you do them?

The problem with discretionary time is that it is not handed to
you in a nicely wrapped package. It comes to you in bits and
pieces—chopped up. It may be 10 or 15 minutes early in the morn-

ing or before you have to dash out for lunch. It may be half an hour at the very end of the day—not a time when you feel like tackling anything important.

The point is that in order to be able to use your discretionary time effectively you have to have it available in big chunks and at a period of the day when you're at a peak in terms of your ability to work efficiently. This is known as "prime time" (see below, page 85). You can't really cope with a complex matter unless you have one-and-a-half or two hours at your disposal.

Getting a slice of time like that, during your workday, may be about as tough as getting two weeks of vacation in mid-January. The best thing to do is schedule it in advance. Before you leave the office on Friday afternoon, pick out a day during the coming week and block out two hours of discretionary time for yourself.

This may or may not work. Your boss may come bursting into your office with a crisis for you to handle. An important customer may call. Other interruptions are likely to occur. In order to make those two hours really worthwhile, you're going to have to insulate or isolate yourself. You're going to have to stay on top of your calendar, get control of the telephone, and learn to say "no".

You may also find valuable blocks of time while traveling or even commuting. You may be able to sleep less and work more intensively during your peak hours. Beating the clock is one of the keys to working smart, and this chapter tells you how you can do it.

KEEPING TRACK

There are many tried and proven tools available to help you manage your time. You can use a personal diary, notebook, large calendar or wall chart. Choose the system that seems to work best for you. The important thing is keeping track, knowing what you have to do when.

Many executives prefer one variation or another of the wall calendar. Its big advantage is that it makes the tracking process visual.

You use the wall calendar to record all of your commitments for as far into the future as possible. This includes not only lunch dates, speaking engagements, seminars and conventions, but also such personal items as birthdays and anniversaries. Use different colored inks, red for business entries, blue for personal ones. Enter tentative commitments in pencil.

Don't merely record the dates of the events but take preparation time into account. For example, if you have to make a presentation at the company sales convention on the 25th, it's a good idea to block out the 23rd and 24th as rehearsal dates.

Check your calendar frequently to get a general idea of what's coming up the week ahead and month ahead. This will prepare you mentally for important events and will also serve to cue you or your secretary to make necessary travel reservations or assemble needed information and materials.

Always consult the calendar before taking on a new commitment. This prevents you from overloading certain weeks, while leaving others relatively uncluttered.

At random times throughout the year, enter a "free day" for yourself. It's a good way to assure you'll get them.

The personal notebook in diary form is a variation of the wall calendar. Its advantage is that you can carry it with you. A disadvantage is that it's not as efficient from a visual standpoint; you can't see an entire month at one time.

AVOIDING INTERRUPTIONS

Let's suppose you've blocked out a big chunk of time in your daily schedule with the idea of tackling a major project, perhaps a report you have to write. A week in advance you enter the time period on your calendar. But when the time arrives, on the day you planned to do the important work, you come under assault immediately. Your boss, a subordinate and a co-worker, all expressing different degrees of urgency, want some of your time. The individual demands aren't especially time consuming, but taken together they're significant. Worse, they destroy your ability to concentrate. What can you do about this all too common situation?

You can't eliminate interruptions. They're as much a part of office life as the coffee break and three-day weekend. What you have to do is evaluate each as it occurs. If the interruption is a telephone call from an important client, your decision will inevitably be to put aside what you're doing and take it. If the call is from your insurance agent, you can probably call back later. As long as you have your priorities clearly established and keep them uppermost in your mind, making decisions regarding interruptions should never be difficult.

Of course, not every interruption is necessarily bad. A chance hallway meeting or random telephone call may offer the opportunity of asking an important question or making a report. Either one is a chance to get something done. Experts in time management call this "unplanned interaction."

As a general rule, however, you have to learn to insulate yourself from unnecessary, unwanted interruptions. A classic example of executive insulation occurred during Franklin D. Roosevelt's second administration. By an executive order issued in 1939, Roosevelt created the Executive Office of the President "to protect the President's time" by "excluding any matter that can be settled elsewhere." This eventually evolved into an army of assistants and advisers who shield the president from the outside world. These people decide what matters should be brought to the president's attention and in what form. In those matters that are to be delegated, they decide who can best handle each, how it should be handled and when it should be completed.

During Ronald Reagan's final years as president, the White House received 50,000 telephone calls a day—30,000 for Reagan himself—and some 12,000 to 20,000 pieces of mail. Handling it took a staff of 59 full-time employees, 33 part-timers and more than 500 volunteers.

Your own staff, minuscule by comparison, should be accomplishing much of what the huge White House staff accomplishes. Your staff—or your assistant or secretary—should insulate you from the outside world.

Your secretary plays the key role. Give him or her the authority to make decisions and solve problems.

Your secretary should screen your mail, handling all routine correspondence. If necessary, draft common replies to the most frequent queries you receive and let your secretary use them as models to follow. Telephone calls should be screened in a similar fashion (page 82).

Your secretary should maintain your appointment schedule, acting to shield you from drop-in visitors. He or she can also be charged with the responsibility of reminding you of important events, even birthdays, anniversaries and the like.

Tell your secretary the principles of organization you use. He or she can then help you stay organized, cooperating with you in the handling of priority items.

Tell your secretary your goals. Use your secretary's decision-making and problem-solving capabilities. Once your secretary feels comfortable in this role, he or she will be able to handle a substantial part of the work that makes up your response time, your fixed time, thus affording you more discretionary time. More important, your secretary can be of exceptional value in helping you to achieve those goals you have set for yourself.

HIDING OUT

Richard Nixon was extremely efficient as a time manager. One of his techniques involved the use of a small private office in the Executive Office Building across the street from the White House. Armed with several yellow legal pads, Nixon would walk over to the office to work alone. His aides were under orders not to interrupt him except in the case of an emergency.

Consider a second office as a means of isolating yourself when you want to concentrate on a major project. The office can be in the same building in which you work, even on the same floor. Maybe it's at home or close to your home. Responding to this need, an entrepreneur in Fairfield County, Connecticut, has erected an office building that provides second offices for Manhattan executives who live in Connecticut.

If a second office is beyond your command, consider your automobile as an alternative. Drive to a quiet spot and do your thinking in the car. Public libraries offer soundproof carrels where individuals can work undisturbed.

John Fanning, chairman of the board and president of Uniforce Temporary Personnel, Inc., gets the privacy he feels he needs by going into the office on Saturday morning. "I like to come in leisurely," he says. "I wear leisure clothes. I read the morning paper, the sports pages, chiefly, for the first half hour or so. Then for the next three or four hours I follow standard operating procedure that's right out of Peter Drucker. I take a legal-size yellow pad and write at the top of it, 'What I can do in a meaningful way to develop Uniforce.' And I write out my ideas. In the last ten years, I may have missed two Saturdays doing this. It's a very enjoyable period for me. I find myself good company in that sense.

"One of the things we're now doing is converting existing temporary-help services to the Uniforce system. It's what *Inc.* magazine has called 'creative reconceptualization.' It's proven to be a bonanza for us. Well, that idea came out of one of those Saturday sessions, from the laboratory, as I call it. I remember that particular Saturday because I wrote non-stop for three or four hours, filling page after page after page.

"Often in this company," says Fanning, "there isn't time for people to think. Everybody is busy working. Somebody better be thinking—and I don't mean consultants, that is, outsiders. It has to be an insider. One person who has a chance to think is me."

You can't say too much about the benefits of quiet time, a time when there are no visitors, no telephone calls—nothing. It's a recess period for your mind. "Privacy," Supreme Court Justice Louis Brandeis once said, "is the right to be alone—the most comprehensive of rights, and the right most valued by civilized man."

THE OPEN DOOR

Some executives try to be available to everybody all the time. They like to say they have an open-door policy. But such a policy is not wise, unless you're in training for a career in local politics. When your door is open to everyone, you're letting other people set your priorities. You are no longer in control of your time. Rather than avoiding interruptions, you're inviting them.

"Everybody loves the open door policy—in principle," says Kevin Daley, president of Communispond. "You'll never hear anyone say it's bad. And, yet, in terms of getting things accomplished, there is nothing more destructive to the senior person.

"If people can come in at any time, which they want to be able to do, they virtually 'invalidate' the person sitting in the corner office."

Instead of closing his office door tightly, Daley sometimes leaves it ajar. "If the door is ajar," he says, "it means, 'Kevin really doesn't want you to come in, but you can if it's important.' "

Another alternative is to establish blocks of time during the day when you're available on a regular basis, a time when subordinates know they will be able to see you. At other times, they will realize, you are available only in the case of some emergency.

You can also try telling subordinates that you'll drop by when asked. Have them call your assistant to make their request. This enables you to maintain control over the get together. You schedule it when it's convenient; you can end it at any time. In addition, you flatter the subordinate by going to his or her office.

Of course, it's possible to establish such policies and still be interrupted occasionally by a drop-in visitor. Anyone who plunks himself or herself down in a chair in your office is likely to shatter your work schedule for the better part of a morning or afternoon.

If you're in the midst of something important, it's best to handle the interruption by saying. "I'm in the middle of something important right now. Can we get together a little later?"

Another solution is to stand up to greet and talk to the interrupter. Maybe you can move the conference into the hallway outside your office. Either way, the conversation is likely to end much more quickly than if you are both seated comfortably.

To discourage drop-in visitors, some executives avoid putting any chair in their offices except their own, or at least limit the number of chairs. The awkwardness of just standing there curbs long visits.

Another method of forestalling such interruptions is to turn your desk around so that your back is to the door. This prevents you from making eye contact with passersby and thus discourages them from greeting you and then dropping in.

The problem here is that your co-workers are going to think of you as being cold and aloof. The solution might be to turn your desk sideways. Then you won't be making that critical eye contact, but you won't be thought of as an unfriendly workaholic.

If the interruptions come from the boss, it's a little trickier. Maybe you can resolve this problem by getting your boss to organize himself or herself. Suggest that the two of you meet twice a day—at 10:30 a.m. and 3 p.m., for instance—to discuss work in progress or assignments the boss might have for you. Then enter these daily meetings on your work schedule.

Interruptions can also be a problem when you seek to work at home. Moving your desk to face in one direction or another is not going to help. Begin by explaining your schedule to your family, then stick to that schedule. If you tell them that you're going to quit work at 9:00 p.m. and spend time with them, then don't fail to live up to that promise.

With kids, reassure them. Explain that you'd rather be doing things with them but your work has a special importance right now. That way they're less likely to feel hurt. They'll also be less inclined to distract you.

SAYING NO

Just as you evolve a To-Do list every day, so should you evolve a Not-To-Do list. Not-To-Do activities are those that you assume in an effort to please someone else; they are really of little or no importance to you. Such involvements can easily wreck your effectiveness. Some people waste hours, even days, on tasks they never should have taken on in the first place.

The problem here is the inability to say no. People often say "yes" when they want to say "no" because they don't want to hurt someone's feelings. Not only do such individuals frequently find themselves overcommitted, but also they end up attending a lot of boring parties and buying things they never intended to buy.

Remember your priorities, what's important to you. Remember, it's your right to say no. You don't have to feel defensive about it. You don't have to offer an excuse.

Practice negative responses. Get into the habit of hearing yourself say them. It may not feel natural at first but it will later, with practice.

In cases where you find yourself wavering, muster enough courage at least not to say "yes." Say, "Let me check my schedule, think about it and get back to you." If you have a couple of hours, or overnight, to ponder the pitfalls involved in accepting an unwanted assignment, you'll be much more likely to eventually generate the courage necessary to deliver a firm "no."

Saying no also applies to telling a superior when a deadline is impossible to meet or his or her demand on your time is excessive. Of course, this doesn't mean that you should refuse to do the task. But you shouldn't remain silent about its difficulty. Perhaps you can bargain with your superior for assistance. "Sure, I can do it," you can say, "but I'd like to hire a couple of temps to help out."

Learning to say no is an acquired skill like learning to ride a bicycle or ice-skate. The more you practice the skill the more proficient you'll become.

GETTING CONTROL OF THE TELEPHONE

As difficult as it is to imagine life without the telephone, there are many days when life *with* the telephone also becomes impossible.

Even with all the advances in telephone technology of recent years (see "High-Tech Telephone Help," page 84), the telephone can still be a terrible timewaster. It's not so much the time you spend on "hold" or getting a busy signal or wrong number. It's the idle conversations that eat up big chunks of time. Look at it like this: Suppose you're involved in 10 calls a day. On each, you spend about five minutes on small talk. That's almost an hour a day you're giving away.

Most people place and accept a total of about 10 calls a day. With sales people, however, 30 to 40 calls is standard. Obviously, learning to limit conversations is essential.

Good telephone management begins from the switchboard and continues with your secretary. He or she should be furnished with a permanent list of people from whom you will always take calls. The secretary should also be provided with a list specifying each project or assignment for which an assistant of yours is responsible, so that he or she can direct calls to the proper individual.

It's also a good idea to establish one or two periods during the day for placing and receiving calls. The best time is the morning, when people are most likely to be in their offices.

Before you place a call, make a list of the key points you want to cover. When you've checked off all of the items, you may want to socialize briefly, but be ready to cut off the conversation as soon as the opportunity arises. You can also try ending a conversation with this technique, "Gee, Gil, I know you must be busy; I can't take any more of your time."

Theatrical producer Alexander Cohen sometimes handles as many as 35 or 40 telephone calls in an hour. At peak periods, he has a receiver in each hand, and then an assistant will come into his office with a hand-lettered sign bearing the name of a third caller, and a second assistant will enter with a second sign and the name of a fourth caller.

"But the calls are easy to handle," Cohen says, "because I've developed a relationship with people so that I can say, 'Harvey, he said yes,' and then immediately hang up. Done. End of conversation.

"I don't have all those other things to go through on the telephone. It's very, very rare that I have a phone call that lasts more than a minute, because I can give you an answer to the question you're asking me, and if I can't answer it, I know who to refer you to. And the converse is true in terms of the information I seek from others. So once you've established relationships with people, and they know the pace at which you work, they realize it."

One good way of helping to assure brief conversations is to place your calls just before lunch or at the end of the day. Most people aren't eager to linger on the telephone during such periods.

If there are certain people who never fail to be longwinded when you call, consider not calling them at all. These are people whom you should try dealing with by letter or memo. Your phone time should be reserved for those who don't waste it.

Friends who remain on the phone for longer than a half hour are probably using you as a substitute therapist, according to Shirley Belz of the National Home Study Council. "Interject some of your own problems," she says, "and you'll soon find they don't have time to talk."

You can help yourself get control of the telephone by having your secretary audit your calls for a week or two. Keep track of who called, when they called, the purpose of the call and the length of time you spent on it. Keep track of your outgoing calls in a similar manner. Once the audit is completed, you can use it to determine whether you're spending unnecessary time on the phone.

HIGH-TECH TELEPHONE HELP

Though what you say and how long you stay on the phone remain up to you, a revolution in telephone technology in recent years has made the telephone a more efficient instrument to dial and transport. A cordless phone, for example, permits you to walk around as you speak. You're never "out of the office." A speaker phone is recommended if you want to do paperwork with your hands while you're handling a call. Automatic dialing can be a good timesaver if you place a lot of calls.

Programmable telephones can store as many as 81 numbers that can be called up from memory and redialed. A screen can be programmed to list the calls to be made on a given day. Automatic paging systems and beepers are popular. Try out different technical innovations, adopting those that suit your needs.

When traveling, be aware that Hertz, Budget, National and some of the other rental firms now offer cellular phones. Charges are modest, less than $10 a day. For the business person who travels in his or her own car, there's Audiotel, a mobile phone with a built-in answering machine. The device can give the caller a number at which the driver can be reached, and also record any messages left by callers.

Air-to-ground telephone service is now available on American, Eastern, TWA, Northwest, Piedmont and several other airlines. Calls can be placed to anywhere in the United States, including Hawaii and Alaska.

In the case of your home phone, a phone machine or an answering service may be useful. Most phone machines are equipped with monitors, which enable you to screen calls.

One person I know refuses to let meals or other important moments at home be interrupted by the telephone's ring. She simply refuses to pick up the phone. "If it's important, they'll call back," she says. "If it's not, they won't. I never feel I've missed anything."

PRIME TIME

There are periods during the day when you are at your peak mentally and physically. You're able to accomplish more with less effort than at any other time of day.

This has to do with the concept of biological rhythm—or biorhythm—still a relatively unexplored process. An individual unwittingly makes reference to the biorhythmic factor by describing himself or herself as a "morning person" or a "night person."

As this suggests, the period of greatest energy and acumen varies from one individual to the next. For me, it is very early in the morning. I like to start writing at somewhere between 4:30 and 5:00 a.m. I write for three or four hours, have breakfast, and then write for another hour or so. Most of the rest of the day is spent preparing for the next morning's writing session, whether I'm working in the library, doing an interview or reading.

My energy level drops in the afternoon after lunch. I wouldn't think of trying to write then. I schedule tasks that don't require great acuity. I might make some telephone calls or do some filing. I find it very easy to doze or even nap during this period.

In the early evening hours, I perk up again. A second drop later on in the evening makes it easy to go to bed.

Richard W. Wallach, a justice of the New York Supreme Court, Appellate Division, who gets up each day at 5 a.m., calls the early-morning hours "the undiscovered gold-mine of the day," according to an article in the *New York Times*. Judge Wallach brews some coffee and then reads. It can be something light or a complex legal case.

Daniel J. Boorstin, the Librarian of Congress, is another individual who has discovered the merits of rising at about the same time as the sun. Dr. Boorstin is at his desk in his home before 6 a.m. "The three or four hours before I go into the library are my best writing hours," Dr. Boorstin told the *Times*. Boorstin won a Pulitzer Prize in 1974 for his book *The Americans: The Democratic Experience*. "There are no engagements you can make at these hours. There are fewer temptations."

Many people whom I know think that this type of schedule is insane. If they should awaken at 5 a.m. or thereabouts, they think they're having an insomnia attack. Some of these people find their energy levels begin escalating around 10 or 11 in the evening. They start working around midnight and keep going until dawn. Other freelancers I know feel perfectly comfortable working a nine-to-five day.

You should determine your own prime time. When is your energy level at its highest? When do you feel the most mentally acute?

You probably already have some idea of your own biorhythmic

pattern. You can bring it into sharper focus by performing some simple experiments at different times during the day.

Suppose you have an important report to write for a client. Arrange your schedule so you can work on one portion of the report in the morning, another portion in the afternoon. Was there any difference in your ability to solve the problems presented by the report? Was your mental sharpness and ability to express yourself higher in the morning or afternoon?

Another experiment calls for taking a fast walk around the block in the morning; do the same in the afternoon. Did one walk leave you feeling refreshed while the other drained you?

When you've worked out a pattern for yourself, draw up a chart showing your daily highs and lows. It might look like this:

7:00 a.m. to 9:00 a.m.	—	Moderate
9:00 a.m. to Noon	—	High
Noon to 3:00 p.m.	—	Moderate
3:00 p.m. to 6:00 p.m.	—	Low
6:00 p.m. to 8:00 p.m.	—	Moderate
8:00 p.m. to 10:00 p.m.	—	High

Arrange to perform your most critical tasks during your prime time. These are the tasks that require the most in the way of concentration and original thought. Arrange to do the tasks that are ordinarily the most stressful during these time periods, too.

When you're at less than your best, try to do routine work—telephoning or signing your correspondence. In the periods when your energy level is at its lowest, schedule some quiet time for yourself. Try sitting at your desk for five or ten minutes with your eyes closed, breathing deeply. You may be surprised at how much this refreshes you.

There are going to be times, of course, when your biorhythmic pattern is in direct conflict with your office schedule. For example, a meeting with an important client will be set for a time when you are in low gear. One thing you can try to do on such occasions is boost your blood sugar level, which is also a factor in how you feel physically and mentally. About 15 minutes before the meeting begins, have a glass of fresh orange juice, a few spoonfuls of cottage cheese or a small handful of nuts. This might do the trick. But it would be better if you could get the meeting rescheduled.

EFFICIENT SLEEP

Most people get the sleep they need. "Still," says Michael J. Thorpy, director of the Sleep-Wake Disorder Center at the Montefiore Hospital in New York City, "a significant percentage of people spend too much time in bed."

According to recent studies, the quantity of time you spend in bed isn't what's important; the quality of sleep you get when you're there is what counts.

Perhaps you can cut back the amount of time you spend in bed. Reducing bed time by just an hour a night would give you the equivalent of another workday every week.

If this idea sounds appealing to you, first try improving the quality of your sleep. Daily exercise—swimming, cycling or light jogging—may help you get more rest from fewer hours in bed. Never exercise later than two hours before bedtime, however.

Your diet is important, too. Avoid such stimulants as caffeine during the day. Some people limit their caffeine to breakfast. It's widely believed that a glass of wine or a bottle of beer helps induce sleep, but the truth is that alcohol actually interferes with sleep, and too much alcohol may trigger insomnia.

Do whatever you can to avoid stressful situations during the day. Tension and anxiety are even worse than caffeine when it comes to trying to get a refreshing sleep.

Make an effort to go to bed at the same time each night and arise at the same time each morning. A relaxing bath just before retiring may help you fall asleep. A glass of warm milk is another tried and proven relaxant. Don't go to bed if you feel wide awake. Read for a while, watch television or listen to some soothing music.

If you want to try to reduce the number of hours you spend

sleeping, begin by keeping a sleep diary for a week or so. For each night, record the time you went to bed and when you awakened in the morning. If you wake up during the night, try to recall the amount of time you remained awake. Also make an assessment of how you felt during the day. Were you alert and efficient? How about your mood, your disposition?

Once you've determined your minimum nightly requirement, begin cutting back in 15 minute segments, either by going to bed 15 minutes later or arising 15 minutes earlier. Try it for a week. If it seems successful, try lopping off another 15 minutes the next week, and so on. Naturally, if you begin feeling fatigued or your efficiency level starts dropping, go back to the previous level.

Most adults sleep between six and eight hours a night. One study reports that the minimum daily requirement if six and one-half hours. But people's needs cover quite a range. Thomas Edison, for example, slept about four hours a night, whereas Albert Einstein slept half the day.

Cutting back on nighttime sleep is not something that should be approached lightly. If you sleep too few hours, fatigue and below par performance are sure to result. Insufficient sleep also leads to crankiness, a quality seldom associated with successful people. The benefits to be derived from an increased amount of daily waking time are obvious, but you should proceed with caution when interfering with your sleep.

USING YOUR TRAVEL TIME

Of the 100 million or so Americans who commute to work, about 84 percent of them travel in private vehicles, spending an average of 23 minutes each way. Those who use public transportation—between six and seven percent—spend twice as much time traveling, about 45 minutes each way. Whether you drive a car to work or hop a commuter train or bus, you're spending the equivalent of several work days every month in commuting. This is time that can be put to good use.

As Jane Meara, author and editor, explains, "When I'm waiting on the platform for the train, I decide what I'm going to read on the way in to New York City, and what I'll read in the evening on the way out. I take a fast look at my newspaper. That's time that's never wasted. I realize that any reading that I do in the hour or so I'm on the train is reading I won't have to do in the evening at home."

If you commute by car, invest in a portable recorder for dictation or a portable cassette player. Educational material is now available on an extraordinary array of prerecorded tapes, everything from Shakespeare's plays to advice on how to become a better public speaker.

You can also listen to tapes or dictate by means of a portable recorder on commuter trains or buses. In addition, you can read or write.

Plan your travel time just as you do your work day. If you spend an hour commuting every day, then provide yourself with an hour's worth of reading, writing, listening or dictating. Over a period of weeks, you can do a mountain of work.

LONG-DISTANCE TRAVEL

Traveling to a distant city may give you an even bigger block of work time—two or three hours in one unit. And it's time in which you're not likely to be subjected to distractions. You may not even *hear* a telephone.

Before your departure, decide what work you're going to do, and get together the materials you're going to need—portable recorder, cassette player, calculator, writing materials. Put everything into your briefcase, which becomes a kind of portable office.

If you are traveling by plane, ask your secretary to reserve you a window seat. There are fewer distractions there. As soon as you are settled in your seat, open up your briefcase and start working.

If you think it would be worthwhile, consider carrying a portable computer terminal with you. Anytime you have access to a telephone, you can "plug in" to your office and go to work. The terminal can be used to turn out typed messages, memos, letters, contracts—anything.

Check in with your office whenever you have a spare moment. Always leave copies of your itinerary with your secretary and at home. This makes you reachable at all times.

· · · · ·

Additional Reading

Getting Things Done; The ABC's of Time Management, by Edwin C. Bliss (Bantam, 1985). A down-to-earth guide for managing your time at the office or at home.

Getting Organized, by Stephanie Winston (Warner, 1985). Focuses on personal organization, everything from meal planning to financial planning.

How to Get Control of Your Life and Time, by Alan Lakein (David McKay, 1973). The noted expert explains how to maximize your productive capabilities; an all-time best-seller.

How to Organize Your Work and Your Life, by Robert Moskowitz (Doubleday, 1981). Tried and proven management techniques for business and professional people.

EXPERT ADVICE

No two people utilize exactly the same time management techniques. What people do differs, like their jobs and personalities. Some people like to get to the office very early; others like to stay late. Some find they get more done by working at home—away from the office distractions—one day each week. Senator William Proxmire saves time by running to work. Norman Vincent Peale finds that his "fractional moments" of work time in cabs, waiting at airports, and the like, add up to considerable blocks of time. *Cosmopolitan* editor Helen Gurley Brown makes sure she's always doing two or three things at once. But Senator Claiborne Pell of

Rhode Island advises focusing on a single problem at a time. Columnist and author William Buckley uses deadlines imposed by his editors as a way of organizing his work time.

The pages that follow offer a collection of "secrets" from these experts and other successful men and women representing a wide range of professions. Although some of the information may not be of any value to you, there are bound to be a few tips that will help you get the most out of the 168 hours you're handed every week.

· · · · ·

Malcolm Forbes

Chairman and chief executive officer, Forbes magazine; author, The Sayings of Chairman Malcolm (Harper & Row, 1978)

There are two things that I do in an effort to get the maximum use out of my working hours. By starting at my desk at 7 a.m., I get two hours of work done without interruption. This is a period of maximum productivity for me.

Second, I am never without a piece of paper and a pencil. I make notes on anything and everything—ideas for editorials, and articles, and things that have to be done. Making notes insures that everything gets covered. You're not constantly saying, "I've got to remember that." If you make a note, you don't have to remember.

· · · · ·

Dina Merrill

Actress

I try not to waste a minute. If I'm riding in a cab, I jot down ideas or make notes of things I have to do. When I travel, I always carry some of my personal stationery with me so I can write notes on airplanes or when I'm waiting in a terminal. I do some of my best thinking when I'm driving a car; as soon as I reach my destination, I put down my ideas on paper. I keep busy, even while I'm waiting for an elevator or to cross a street, by doing isometric exercises.

. . . . .

Julius W. Lang
Management consultant, J. W. Lang/Associates

Managers often need to consolidate their discretionary time into a solid chunk of usable time. You can't accomplish a big job with small scraps of time. How can you get discretionary time under control? There are several ways. Some managers work at home one day a week. This is becoming more and more common. Other managers allot two specific days each week to meetings and problem sessions, and set aside the other days for working on major tasks. Still other managers do all the less important things first, hoping their discretionary time won't be "blown away" by the wind of trivia.

. . . . .

Helen Gurley Brown
Editor, *Cosmopolitan*; author, *Having It All* (Pocket Books, 1983), *Sex and the Single Girl* (Avon, 1983; first published 1963)

My secret for saving time is never, never not to be doing two or possibly three things at once. I'm doing my stomach and face exercises while watching the movie, editing manuscripts in the taxi or on the bus, doing really serious work on any flight from Los Angeles to New York or vice versa, and if I can't actually do anything, I am at least thinking ahead. I stay out of stores . . . you can save thousands of hours in a lifetime that way, though you miss some of the pleasure of looking at pretty stuff. I talk to people on the phone instead of letting them come to see me . . . 20 times out of 21, they want something that wouldn't be possible anyway, and we save each other's time. I would no more let somebody come to see me who hadn't told me what it was about ahead of time than I would let a doctor snatch out my tonsils without a pre-consultation. I watch television (the *Today* show) while I exercise for an hour in the morning, try never to do anything myself that someone who is better at it than I, or paid to do it, can do for me . . . the truth is, I probably need to learn how to relax with some of the time I save!

. . . . .

F. Lee Bailey
Attorney

I am able to carry on my several enterprises (practicing law, speaking, writing, business, etc.) by fine tuning the efficiency of each operation, delegating responsibility effectively to others, maintaining a high level of communications in all areas, and using my own efforts in a way to maximize output without forever burning the midnight oil.

Perhaps most important, I try to stay abreast of the latest that modern technology has to offer, and to utilize that technology to advantage. At the moment, I carry a Toshiba 1100 lap-top IBM-compatible computer with me most of the time, which interfaces with larger computers in every office. Whenever I am traveling—which is most of the time—I am able to use the time involved, whether it be on my own aircraft or an airliner, to accomplish a great deal. The majority of my time is spent with word processing, with spread-sheets and data bases a close second. When I reach my destination, I am able to send by modem the work product to the appropriate office or offices for transcription and distribution. These offices include communications central in Washington, and law offices in Boston, New York, West Palm Beach, Miami and Los Angeles.

I also enjoy excellent telephone communications, recently enhanced by virtue of the cellular mobile network now available in most major cities. The portable Motorola unit I carry works in cars, on boats, and in aircraft. Since the range from an aircraft is considerable because of the altitude, I am almost never out of touch. Once again, time that would otherwise be wasted while on the move becomes productive, since telephone communications are critical to all of my activities. Although the Motorola was expensive ($4,000), it has paid for itself many times over in the sixteen months that I have owned it.

Additionally, I think that my training (both in aviation and in the trial courts) in making swift decisions, and in causing them to be implemented without "going to committee," makes my business life much easier than the lives of many of my colleagues. While it is impossible to make a multitude of decisions on a regular basis without expecting some flaws somewhere, too often failure can be traced to the lack of a decision, or an unwarranted hesitation. In the flying business especially, that can be a terminal shortcoming.

Finally, since my early days as a student (perhaps out of a kind of laziness, initially) I have made an effort to accomplish tasks with a single effort. I do a great deal of organizing in my head before verbalizing. I deliver speeches with no outline and no notes, write a first draft that is usually final except for correcting typos, and cross-examine witnesses for an hour or more without ever referring to a piece of paper, maintaining constant eye-contact in the process. Many people consider such a "modus operandi" to be too difficult. Most of these people have simply failed to comprehend and discipline themselves to fully use the capacity of the human mind to concentrate and memorize.

. . . . .

William Proxmire

U.S. Senator (Wisconsin)

The principal unique system I have for saving time is that I run to work. This enables me to combine commuting, exercising and weight control all in one 35-minute period. Of course, it helps that I have a locker room and shower facilities available at my job, but it's a great way to save time.

. . . . .

Joan Barthel
▲▲▲▲▲▲▲▲▲▲▲▲▲▲▲▲▲▲▲▲▲

Author, A *Death in Canaan* (Dutton, 1976), A *Death in California* (Congdon & Weed, 1981)

I am not a well organized person ordinarily. But when I'm doing a book, I get up real early in the morning to work on it. When I was writing *Death in California,* I got up at four in the morning, and then I just worked all the time, including weekends.

I'd work each day until five or six in the afternoon, then make dinner for my daughter Annie. I'd go to bed early. I never like to write at night; a lot of writers do, I know. But I never like to work after dark. But I would take some notes with me and read them in bed until I fell asleep.

Then I'd get up at four the next morning. It's really a matter of stretching the day by getting up at four instead of seven, my usual time. I'd work for three hours, get Annie up, off to school, and then go right back to the typewriter. By 10 or 11 o'clock in the morning I had put in a full day. It was like I was working double days. That's what it amounted to.

I find that it worked really well, getting work done before the rest of the world wakes up. It didn't take me long to get into the habit. It helped, of course, that I loved the project so much. This sounds real gushy—but I looked forward to getting to the type-writer each morning. I loved the story and putting all the pieces together. I don't think I would have worked with such enthusiasm if I had been doing a bunch of different articles. This was a focused project in which I was really wrapped up.

· · · · ·

John Fanning

Chairman of the board and president, Uniforce Temporary
Personnel, Inc.; author, *Work When You Want to Work* (Pocket
Books, 1985)

I usually arrive at the office between nine o'clock and nine-fifteen.
I try to leave by six or six-thirty. There are a certain number of
hours I feel I have to put in each day.

The business lunch is the most productive part of the day for
me. I take an hour or an hour-and-a-half, but I don't watch the
clock. Rosemary Maniscalco, our executive vice-president, and I
have lunch together. We're a team. We usually accomplish more
in that one hour than in any other hour of the day.

It's informal but we have an agenda. Ninety-eight percent of
the time is spent on business discussion, two percent on personal
matters. We go through the niceties. "How's your mother?" I'll
say. "Is she feeling better?" Things like that. But the real purpose
of the lunch is business.

At lunch, we don't have the damn phone ringing, which is
always a big problem. I find I can't always shut off the phone.
There are certain calls I have to take; I have no choice.

· · · · ·

Art Buchwald

Columnist; author, *While Reagan Slept* (Fawcett, 1984), *You
Can Fool All of the People All of the Time* (Putnam, 1985)

To save time I read in the bathroom.

. . . . .

Ed McMahon
Television emcee

One of the most important secrets of managing your time is to always be on time. There is nothing worse than wasting someone else's time by being late. It is also a tremendous help to have a very efficient assistant, which I have in Madeline Kelly, who places me in the right place at the right time with the right equipment. I learned years ago by being a Marine to always be on time, always be ready, and have the right equipment to do what you're supposed to do when you arrive.

. . . . .

Claiborne Pell
U.S. Senator (Rhode Island)

My only advice with regard to conserving time is to focus on a single problem until it is resolved or the decision is made to put it aside. Never try to solve more than one problem at once.

. . . . .

Richard Adler
Composer/lyricist

I work—creatively speaking—in the morning between 9 a.m. and 1 p.m. I shut off the telephone, and the mail gets delivered to the box outside my studio. I don't want any distractions when I'm writing.

The afternoon I set aside for what I call administrative tasks—

if I have a legal problem, an accountancy problem or something to discuss, public relations or whatever.

I believe in discipline. I swim or run almost every day. Swimming and running are among my priorities. I do these in the morning or afternoon whenever I have a spare hour.

· · · · ·

Marvin Mitchelson

Celebrity lawyer

I'm a workaholic and love my work. My "secret" for managing my time is to work almost around the clock, seven days a week, including holidays.

· · · · ·

Clive Cussler

Author, *Raise the Titanic* (Bantam, 1980), *Pacific Vortex* (Bantam, 1983), *Deep Six* (Simon & Schuster, 1984), *Cyclops* (Simon & Schuster, 1985)

I'm probably the last guy who'd be considered to replace Lee Iacocca. Efficiency has never exactly been my greatest talent. During my days working for other people and corporations (advertising copywriter), the biggest organizational priority was simply meeting a deadline; creativity was something else again. So I wasn't a whiz at accounting for every minute of the day.

Now, however, being my own boss, I have swamped myself in work and extracurricular activities I enjoy, it suddenly becomes necessary to organize.

There is the writing, at least six hours a day. My car collection takes around six hours a week. And my shipwreck research, planning and expeditions take place about three times a year. Then there is the management of real estate, publishers and agent, and correspondence.

My secret? With my mundane I.Q. of 124 I had to come up with something simple and easy. And I did.

After I wake up in the morning, I stare at the ceiling for twenty minutes, scheduling out the day, outlining the next chapter to write, and figuring the priorities of who and what comes first in regard to appointments, letters and phone calls. I keep it all in my head without notes which would take the fun out of it all with excess rigidity. Oh sure there are interruptions. My daughter will come by with the grand kids, unexpected calls, the gardener can't make it till next week, the toilet plugs up, and my wife has to have her allotment of nagging. But that all comes with the territory when you work at home.

I wish I could give you an exotic, and for that matter, erotic, secret for managing time, but that's it.

. . . . .

Liv Ullman

Actress

My schedule is such that I'm unable to devote time to any projects other than the ones I'm already committed to at this moment.

I guess that is my "secret"—learning to say no to so many projects, many of which I would like to become a part of.

. . . . .

Eliot Janeway

President, Janeway Publishing and Research Corporation; author, *Prescriptions for Prosperity* (Times Books, 1983)

I try to separate my work between targeting people and paper. My purpose is to divide my time and energy between lining up phone calls or correspondence or meetings and focusing on serious writing.

The former exercise is staccato and involves business awaiting disposal; the latter commands the concentration required to meet disciplined standards and produce serious work of an enduring character.

· · · · ·

Jane Meara

Author, *Growing Up Catholic* (Doubleday, 1986); associate editor, Beech Tree Books (William Morrow & Co.)

I'm a great list maker. Lists save the day for me. I'd go stark raving mad trying to juggle in my mind everything I have to do. I find that when I write something down on a list, it's as good as done.

I make lists of work things, lists of book things, and lists of personal things. I try to keep them separate from one another as much as I can. My life is organized into categories as much as possible. That way I don't mix up obligations that are unrelated to one another.

I try to schedule myself every day. But I'm a very rebellious person. I find the harder I try to force myself to do X at the time I've alloted for X, and do Y at the time I've planned for Y, the more I rebel. So I find that over-scheduling doesn't work. I end up staring at the four walls and getting nothing done. So I try to organize my life in a less formal manner.

I try to casually set up time in my mind as to when I'm going to deal with things. I usually do that in the morning. I go into the office five days a week and I have the kind of a job that demands a lot of work at home as well, reading, mostly. That's pretty much a constant in my life, an obligation I have to live with seven days a week.

I usually stay in the office as late as I can. It's quiet time because the phones stop ringing. I do some of the things that I'd otherwise have to do at home during this time in the peace of a closed-down office. I also do a lot of work riding back and forth on my commuting train from Long Island to New York City.

I use every possible moment. I try not to let any wasted time enter my day.

As soon as I get home, I decide what work I have for my job that is imperative and that I must do, and I'll do that as soon as I get home. In an hour, or an hour-and-a-half, that work is completed and out of my life.

Then what I do—and this may seem really silly—is straighten up my house. That kind of clears the decks for me. I walk around the house and hang up coats and put dishes in the dishwasher. Things like that. I find it's much easier to work in a neat environment. I don't want to have to look up and think, "Oh, God, I have to do the dishes!" I try to get all of my little day-to-day obligations out of my way. My mind is then clear to turn to new things—like my book writing, which I usually do from nine to twelve.

The most important thing in juggling all of these things is keeping them distinct from one another. I don't go back and forth from one to the other. I need to completely remove my job from my mind to do my book work, and vice versa.

I work about three days a week on whatever book project I have—two evenings during the week, and one full day on weekends.

I keep the schedule somewhat flexible. My job at the office is very demanding. There are some manuscripts that have to be read right away. So the weekdays that I work on my own book can be any two days.

I wish I was one of those people who gets up at five o'clock in the morning, two hours before breakfast. But when I wake up in the morning, I feel the responsibilities of the day really weighing upon me, and I can't give my whole attention to my writing. I'm thinking of the things I have to do in the office that day—what things I have to read, what things I have to edit, what people I have to meet with and who I'm having lunch with. I don't have a clear head. I find that it's only at the end of the day when my daily obligations are finished, and my house is in order, that I feel mentally free to tackle my writing.

I set myself up a little room at home. It has nothing in it but my typewriter and a table. There's nothing in there to remind me of all the other things I have to do.

. . . . .

Edward A. Gee
Retired chairman, International Paper Company

I would say three things are of primary importance to an executive.

First, a good secretary, who understands you and your job, is an essential ingredient. One who can discard or reroute the 95% "chaff" that flows to an executive office and pass to you the remaining "wheat." One who keeps you on calendar, on time, and who has that seventh sense about the priority of visitors and more importantly of telephone calls.

Second, an ability to delegate whenever practical. This includes decisions as well as correspondence. Not only does this save your time, but encourages and develops staff.

Finally, for those items that are yours alone to decide, answer or review, do it immediately. Don't set them aside for that free moment of contemplation that never comes; don't let piles of memorandums and reports accumulate in your office for that weekly glance; and don't delay unduly the difficult and the complex. Nothing wastes more time, personal or organizational, than a vacillating executive.

. . . . .

Gregory McDonald
Author, Fletch & the Man Who (Warner, 1983), Fletch Won (Warner, 1985), Flynn's In (Warner, 1985)

The thing I've discovered essential to my work is: always plan out and even start tomorrow's work before finishing today's. This eliminates the terror of the blank page.

· · · · ·

Ted Key
Cartoonist

As a freelance cartoonist and writer, I *never* wait for inspiration. I sit at my drawing board, or typewriter, at a specific time each morning and work a minimum of eight hours. On good days, I turn out a lot of product—good, bad or indifferent. On bad days, less product—good, bad or indifferent. The quality and quantity seem to average out.

When completing a long-term project (such as a screen story), I send the manuscript to the decision makers and go to work *immediately* on another long-term project. By the time I receive an acceptance, or rejection, almost all of my emotions are invested in the new project. Rejection can often knock the wind out of one's sales (sails). But not if you're in love with what you're currently doing.

· · · · ·

Jim Davis
Cartoonist; author, Here Comes Garfield (Ballantine, 1984), Garfield Weighs In (Ballantine, 1984), Garfield Makes It Big (Ballantine, 1985)

I surround myself with people who can take care of the details of business to enable me to concentrate on writing, playing a round of golf, or browsing through wine books. Also, getting an early start on the day, about 6:00 a.m., helps. So does being an insomniac.

. . . . .

John Glenn
▲▲▲▲▲▲▲▲▲▲▲▲▲▲▲
Astronaut, Mercury 6; U.S. Senator (Ohio)

About the only unusual time-saver I find is making use of time spent in the automobile. In Thoreau's day, people apparently sought out their individual Walden ponds to stroll about while doing their best thinking, but I find in my case the automobile, commuting to and from the office, has become my Walden pond, for it seems to be the only time I am truly alone and thinking about a number of things but still have to be sufficiently alert and active to drive the automobile. As a result, I keep either a tape recorder or a note pad on the seat beside me, and make numerous notes and ideas for things which will later remind me of the particular thought or project. I have done that for many years and find it very useful.

. . . . .

Tom Bradley
〰〰〰〰〰〰〰〰〰〰〰〰〰〰
Mayor of Los Angeles

There are a few situations during which I try to keep working, no matter what, even though it may be unconventional. For example, I always take either reading material, letters or speeches along in the car, on the way to various meetings or events. This allows me to visit many areas of our physically large city, but at the same time to preserve all the "office" time I can.

Another situation during which I try to keep working is mealtime. I attempt to maintain my work pace either by reading while eating, or by holding meetings—formal or informal—during meals.

Of course, delegation of authority is one of the most important elements of time-saving. Relying upon staff members whose judgment I trust saves me enormous amounts of time in preparation for decision-making.

In addition, I try not to waste any time during my evenings, and I often return to the office following social events or dinners. This often allows me to get a start on the next day's work.

. . . . .

Toni Stabile

Author, *Cosmetics*: *The Great American Skin Game* (Charter, 1979), *Everything You Want to Know About Cosmetics* (Dodd, Mead, 1984)

Everything I wear is filed. I have my dresses arranged in groups, long-sleeved, short-sleeved, sleeveless; coats, suits and jackets according to weights. My dressy and/or crushable blouses are hung separately according to color and sleeve length; others are folded in plastic bags and in drawers marked according to fabric, color and sleeve length. Sweaters are separated into drawers marked "cardigans" and "pullovers," and then according to sleeve length, color and fiber, such as wool or cotton. Even my hosiery is separated and labeled "toes" or "sandals" and color group.

I believe in impulse buying and making it a practice never to go just shopping, but to incorporate a pass through stores on my way to or from an appointment, or any time out. If I see something I really like and I have enough money to pay for it, I add it to my collection just as a numismatist adds to his coin collection.

When I want something to wear, I "shop my closet." It's less time consuming than store shopping.

I don't make a big deal about having the "right" outfit for a particular occasion any more. I used to, but it always seemed to rain when I expected the sun to shine, or the day heated up when I was ready for arctic winds—and I'd have to scramble for alternatives. I still believe in having my clothes, accessories and wallet in order the night before. But I also know that I can pull together something from my closet or bureau drawers that will see me through.

. . . . .

Norman Vincent Peale
〰〰〰〰〰〰〰〰〰〰〰〰〰〰〰〰〰〰〰〰〰〰〰〰〰〰〰〰〰

Clergyman; author, *The Power of Positive Thinking* (Fawcett, 1973; first published 1952), *You Can If You Think You Can* (Fawcett, 1978), *The True Joy of Positive Living; An Autobiography* (Morrow, 1984)

I guess my first secret is "organization." This means that you take one thing at a time and give it your undivided attention. My wife tells me that I have the capacity to block out noise, confusion, almost anything that is going on around me if I need to concentrate to get a job done.

My second secret is to be able to change the pace. If a solution does not come or a piece of writing does not flow or the preparation of a speech does not jell, I leave it and take a walk or read a mystery story or find some physical work to do. Often the idea I have been searching for will pop up in my mind during such an interim. I have often advised tense and busy businessmen to drop everything and walk one-half mile. I have had some very interesting testimonies of the effectiveness of this plan.

Third, I have always used fractional moments—such as riding in a taxi, waiting in an airport, a plane trip, etc. These add up into a considerable block of time per day. During these fractional moments I can put down a speech outline, plan an article, lay out a job, which has saved me hours and allowed me to keep up a production schedule.

. . . . .

William F. Buckley
〰〰〰〰〰〰〰〰〰〰〰〰〰〰〰〰〰〰〰〰〰〰〰〰〰〰〰〰

Columnist; editor, *National Review*; author, *Overdrive*: A *Personal Documentary* (Doubleday, 1983), *The Story of Henri Tod* (Doubleday, 1984), *The Temptation of Wilfred Malachey* (Workman, 1985).

I am dominated by deadlines. Whatever needs to be done to fulfill a deadline, is what tends to be done. Beyond that, I have only this to add: that any writer makes a terrible mistake in failing to do just that, meet his deadlines. In my experience, he elongates his work unnecessarily (there obviously are exceptions.)

. . . . .

Tom Johnson

Publisher and chief executive officer, Los Angeles Times

Here are two general rules I attempt to follow. When I do, it reduces my work load immensely.

When practical, take the phone call *when it comes through.* (This saves a vast amount of time in trying to reconnect with the caller through return calls, leaving word, etc.)

Handle incoming mail only once. That is, respond to the letter immediately after you read it—unless research or further evaluation is required. A letter which goes back into the "in" basket means you must work that item more than once, actually often doubling the time dedicated to it.

. . . . .

Leo Buscaglia, PhD

Author, Personhood (Fawcett, 1982), Living, Loving, Learning (Fawcett, 1983), Loving Each Other (Slack, 1984), Love (Fawcett, 1986)

There is no "secret" for time management. You must just keep in mind that it's limited, that no amount of money in the world can buy it, and that it's ours to use or abuse—whichever we choose.

4

More
Tips for
Working Smart

~~~~~~

*Getting organized is not merely a matter of develop-
ing and pursuing certain management techniques. It
can also refer to your tools—your desk and how you
use it, your office implements and supplies. It has to
do with your working environment and whether it
encourages effectiveness and efficiency. It has to do
with how you handle meetings, too often the bane of
office workers' lives.*

The tools you use should be suited to your personality and temperament. "You have to get the physical things matched to the way you function," says Denslow Brown of New York, a professional organizer for more than a decade.

"For some people," says Brown, "a file box containing 3" × 5" cards is just perfect for keeping track of things. They just love it. But to others, it means nothing. It'll sit on their desk and never get used and wind up being discarded. Other people need a lot of table space. They need things spread out. Putting things away doesn't work for them. They want everything visual."

An organizational system that works for one person can cause chaos for another, says Brown, whose clients include authors, lawyers, artists, musicians, university professors, film producers and business executives. "I hate to read articles on time management that say, 'This is how you should do this, or this is how you should do that,' " she says. "If something works for you, no matter how chaotic it might seem to others, leave it as it is. On the other hand, don't be blind to the seriousness of the problem if you can't find your desk under the rubble."

Brown describes herself as an "office supply store junkie." She's forever poking through such stores to see what's new and different. She advises her clients to do the same. "We've had a breakthrough in office supplies," she says. "There are amazing things out there. You can make a tremendous improvement in your life just by getting a good calendar."

Of course, getting organized means more than merely acquiring the right tools—the physical level of organization. There are also emotional and behavioral levels.

Organization on an emotional level, according to Denslow Brown, has to do with figuring out what's going on in your work environment. "Ask yourself, 'Why am I allowing clutter and disorganization to sabotage my work?' "

The behavioral level has to do with the willingness to get your body and mind to perform a given task this way instead of that way, the willingness to change bad habits. It has to do with the willingness to use the tools and consult wall charts and calendars that can help you get and stay organized.

If you feel that getting organized is a task beyond your capabilities, take heart—help is available. There are about 100 professionals who now operate organizational businesses across the country. You can have one come to your office or home to help you make order out of chaos. To get the names and addresses of the professional organizers in your area, send a self-addressed, stamped envelope to the National Association of Professional Organizers (5350 Wilshire Blvd., P.O. Box 36E02, Los Angeles, CA 90036).

"I try to teach my clients not to despair," say NAPO President Maxine Ordesky, who operates The Creative Organizer and Creative Closets in Beverly Hills, California. "Everyone can have some form of organization; no one is impossible."

CHOOSING A DESK

Your desk is your command post. If you have any say as to its size and style, give very serious thought to these matters.

Forget for the moment the desks that are available from your firm's office furniture supplier. All you really need is a surface on which to write. Try to visualize the work area that would best suit your own particular work style.

"I try to convince people to be really eccentric when it comes to choosing a desk. I like to sit up in bed using it, spreading papers everywhere. People should try to think how they can be different from the norm. But it takes a long time to get people to see themselves as unique."

Some people want an absolutely clear surface when they work. Others like to have everything they need at their fingertips. Your desk should reflect your preference.

Desk height is important, too. Manufacturers turn out desks in standard heights, usually 28 or 29 inches. "But people aren't of 'standard' size," says Denslow Brown. People who are shorter or taller than average should work at a desk of appropriate height.

"Some of my clients don't like being seated at a desk," Brown says. "They want to work standing up. So they order a custom-made desk or table that allows them to do so."

If your choice of a desk is limited to what your company's supplier has to offer, you still may have several options. Free-standing pedestal desks are the most widely used style. At its simplest, this type of desk takes the form of a hollow-core door mounted atop a pair of 28-inch high file cabinets. Each file cabinet contains two to four storage drawers.

If you find that this type of desk doesn't offer enough work space and storage, you can choose the "executive L." In this, a table and a storage cabinet are attached at right angles. It's a good arrangement if you like to spread out and have files and records handy.

Another way of increasing both work space and storage space is to use a matching credenza. These are very popular today. Usually the same length as the desk but of shallower depth, the credenza is designed for placement against a wall in front of a window.

Credenzas offer the same drawer options as desks. They're an excellent place for the telephone or a computer terminal.

Desk Chairs. Once you've decided upon a writing surface that's compatible to the way in which you work, the next step is to select a chair. Again, approach the subject with an open mind. The chair takes a wide range of forms, and you should have one that maximizes your ability to sit and work as long as you need to without stress.

Chairs are frequently status symbols. Executive chairs, for example, often have thronelike qualities, their high backs framing the sitter against a background of rich leather or expensive upholstery. They overpower every other chair in their vicinity.

Secretarial chairs, on the other hand, usually small and armless, are meant to look unimportant. Ironically, secretarial chairs have traditionally been better designed for sitting on than over-sized, over-padded executive chairs.

Design should be your basic consideration when you're choosing a chair (unless you're planning to use it as a power symbol, in which case appearance takes preeminence). The seat height should be adjustable so that when you are seated your feet rest flat on the floor. They should not have the slightest tendency to dangle.

Nor should there be any pressure on the underside of your thighs. If you find yourself crossing your legs frequently, it could be to relieve some under-leg pressure. There should be some space between the front edge of the seat and the back of your knees; otherwise, your lower legs will fall asleep.

Check the seat cushion. It should be soft enough to provide some comfort but firm enough to prevent you from sinking down into it.

It's vital that the small of your back be in contact with the chair back so as to support the lumbar region, the lowest segment of the spine. You want your spine to retain its natural curvature as you sit. And you want firm support, meaning the chairback should not be so padded it's soft. If the chair doesn't provide the support you need, a backache is almost sure to result.

Check the armrests, too. They should be long enough to support your forearms and wrists, but short enough so your fingers don't get squeezed beneath the desk's underside. Armrests are often adjustable in height.

Try chairs of several different styles. Try to spend as much time as possible sitting in each before reaching a final decision.

Lighting. The lighting of your office is another topic you should think about. The area where you work should be the best-lit surface in the office. Hot spots of light elsewhere—from a ceiling fixture, for instance—inpede your ability to concentrate and can even cause fatigue. Hot spots can also be caused by light that reflects from the glossy surface of your desk, from the work you've placed there (which is probably white), or from a CRT screen or computer keyboard.

Careful positioning of lights will do away with hot spots. Moving your desk is another solution. Non-reflective desk tops of wood or leather also reduce glare.

Another strategy for alleviating eyestrain is to reduce the amount of contrast between your work and the desk top. Background illumination or a better selection of fixtures (see below) will help in this regard.

Daylight is the most pleasing and effective light source, but even in those offices that have sufficient window space and the right exposure one can rely on daylight for only a few hours. You have to choose between fluorescent and incandescent. Fluorescent does not produce strong shadows and thus is splendid for lighting the broad area of your desk top. But the bluish light cast by fluorescent is unflattering to people and spaces.

Fluorescent is sometimes chosen because it's economical, delivering a relatively large amount of light for each watt of power consumed. Fluorescent tubes have a longer life span than incandescent bulbs. And fluorescent, being cool, does not compete with office air conditioning systems.

Although incandescent is less efficient than fluorescent, it produces a "warm" light that is easier to control as a light source. Many designers combine the two types of light so as to obtain the benefits of each, using fluorescent to light the desk top and incandescent to "wash" the walls or as background lighting elsewhere in the office.

When it comes to lighting your work, what designers call "task lighting," you may have a choice between a pendant fixture, which is suspended above the desk, usually from the ceiling, or a desk lamp. The advantage of the pendant fixture is that it doesn't take up any desk space. Many people prefer the desk lamp, however, because you can adjust it to reduce glare. Track lighting may be another choice. Sometimes a pendant fixture can be suspended from a track to light a desk top.

WORKING AT YOUR DESK

Do whatever you can to make your work environment as productive as possible. If you work in an office behind a desk, you should never do anything at the desk that is unrelated to your work. Don't socialize from behind the desk. Don't take breaks there. When you want to relax with a soft drink or a cup of coffee, move someplace else, even if it involves only sitting in a guest chair in the office. The idea, of course, is through usage and habit to establish a certain character for the desk. It's where work is performed. Period.

Making the desk exclusively a work area will help you in focusing your attention upon the problem at hand. Your mind will be much less likely to wander.

You can also improve your ability to concentrate by always "thinking on paper." Have a pencil in your hand when you think. Jot down whatever thoughts cross your mind. They may be represented by only a fragment of a sentence or even simply a word or two. It doesn't matter. Almost anything you put down serves as an extension of the creative process. Later, by evaluating what you've written, you will be able to clarify your thoughts and expand upon them.

The only papers to keep on your desk are those that relate to the matter on which you're working. Everything else should be put away.

There are some business people who don't agree with this advice. They look upon a cluttered desk as a sign of genius. Harold Geneen, the legendary former head of ITT, boosted the cause of cluttered desks in his book, *Managing*. If you're a leader he said, "you are going to have 89 things on your desk, ten others on the floor beside you and eight others on the credenza behind you." This, Geneen contended, enabled you to grab the information you needed when you needed it.

This system may have worked for Geneen but most people are better served by a clear desk. A cluttered desk is said to indicate a cluttered mind. If you have countless piles of paper stacked on the top of your desk, you're going to have difficulty concentrating on the day's agenda, on what's important. Your eyes will stray around the desk, spot a pile, and you'll want to dip into it. Your attention will be diverted from whatever should be No. 1 at that moment.

If your desk is now cluttered, consider a complete reorganization. Remove everything from the top of the desk and empty all the drawers. Put back only the essential items, those you need within easy reach. You don't need that clock within easy reach; put it on a nearby table or cabinet. You don't need that plant.

The deep drawers in the desk should be given over to a filing system. In them keep information relating to the projects on which you're currently working.

Most office-management specialists recommend two stacked

file trays be placed in one corner of the desk. Incoming paper is collected in one; processed paper—outgoing paper—goes in the other.

MEETINGS

When it comes to things that frustrate men and women in the business world, meetings run a close second to interruptions. While a meeting can be an efficient means of accomplishing several different kinds of tasks, many meetings are too long, too disorganized and too boring to be truly productive. "At one point, I had a firm policy of trying to avoid all meetings whenever and wherever I could," says Robert Moskowitz in his book, *How to Organize Your Work and Your Life.* Moskowitz later yielded somewhat, agreeing to accept about 10% of meeting invitations. But he remained very wary of them. A good meeting, he said, is one he himself runs.

As this suggests, never call a meeting if there might be an alternative method of handling the problems. Perhaps a conference call is the solution. Maybe the job can be done by an individual.

What are the hallmarks of what is likely to be an effective and productive meeting? It will start on time with everyone present and prepared, and it will follow a written agenda. There will be plenty of discussion of the important points, with everyone participating. The meeting will end with a general agreement and with all participants aware of what each is to do as a result of the meeting.

Seek to achieve these characteristics whenever you are called upon to organize a meeting. Keep the number of people attending the meeting as small as possible. It usually follows that the more people you have, the more cumbersome the meeting.

If you don't intend to chair the meeting, select a leader who will run it in a democratic fashion, encouraging everyone to participate. He or she should have the ability to control the meeting and be high enough on the ladder to be able to make decisions and delegate assignments.

Circulate an agenda in advance of the meeting to all of those who will be attending. The agenda should include a statement of the meeting's objective and the topics to be covered. You might also suggest background reading for the participants. This helps to assure that they'll discuss the topics raised intelligently. There'll be less talking around the subject, a malady that besets many meetings. Announce when the meeting is to begin and end.

Stick to the starting and ending times. If some people haven't arrived when the bell rings, start without them. Some managers schedule meetings before lunch or toward the end of the day. This ploy helps to prevent the meeting that dribbles on endlessly.

Begin by announcing the purpose of the meeting, stating clearly what it is intended to achieve. Be aware that problems may arise during the meeting that prevent you from achieving the goal or goals you set. You may have to modify your objectives as the meeting unfolds. In other words, be ready to compromise.

Stick to the agenda, always focusing on the purpose of the meeting. Beware of such timewasters as the raising of topics that have little or nothing to do with the subject under discussion. Beware of gossip and chitchat. Get things back on the track with an assertive but good-humored comment, perhaps something such as, "I know this is fascinating, but if we all don't want to be late for lunch, let's move ahead."

Sometimes a meeting will get stalemated between two opposing points of view. When you begin hearing a succession of sentences beginning with the words, "Yes, but . . . ," it's an indication that two parties are in contention. Don't let such discussions continue interminably. Impose a time limit, perhaps suggesting a group discussion of the topic at the meeting's end.

Even worse are indications of serious conflict or hostility, evidenced by sniping or sarcasm. Such feelings usually have little to do with the meeting and its purpose and may arise from serious personality conflicts. Never allow a meeting to become a forum for such conflicts. Any attempts to resolve conflict should be conducted in private.

When you chair a meeting, it's your responsibility to try to get everyone involved. If some people have failed to speak on a topic, ask them for an opinion.

Someone should be present at the meeting to take the relevant minutes. These should be recorded and duplicated and distributed to participants as soon after the meeting as possible.

When you attend meetings, be prepared. Write down what you want to get out of the meeting.

When you speak, be precise in covering the points you want to make. Jot down a list of key words that relate to the topics you want to cover, and refer to the list when it's your turn to speak. When you've said what you intended to say, stop.

Most of your meeting time will be spent on listening. Take notes on what each participant says. The notes will help you in coming to understand each person's point of view. They'll also be useful when you want to reply to points any individual has made.

There are likely to be times when you feel you're attending too many meetings. Not only are they disrupting your daily work schedule, but you're getting little out of them in terms of accomplishment. When this happens, start sending a representative, someone who will express your ideas and report on what other people have said. You can also avoid unproductive meetings by keeping in contact with the attendees, exchanging ideas and attitudes with them. You may be able to accomplish some of your goals through telephone conversations and hallway exchanges.

THE AUTOMATED OFFICE

Late in the 19th century, the telegraph, telephone and typewriter revolutionized office work. A comparable revolution is taking place today. It involves more than merely computers and computer-related technologies. The office of the future will be an electronically integrated office, providing the means to link computers, telephones, typewriters, photocopiers and other such machines with each other and the outside world. The result will be greater productivity at less cost.

Take the word processor, for instance. It provided for a quantum leap in the output of the average typist. But second generation word processors do much more. They are communicating word processors—CWPs. They can "talk" to other computers through telephone and satellite lines. They can call up information from remote data bases, distribute documents and messages to multiple users and act as a file for personal schedules. And any microcomputer can easily access material held by a CWP.

Big things are happening to the telephone, too. Northern Telephone's Displayphone is a good example. It is actually a microcomputer terminal, integrating the telephone and computer into one desktop unit. It can be connected to almost any line-computer, telephone or other. It has a video screen and touch-sensitive keypad. It can keep watch over your personal schedule and call up the schedules of other people. It can slot in meetings at times when all are free. It can store messages; it can handle electronic mail. No wonder it is being called the "super-controller" of the office of the future.

The filing system continues to be a problem in many offices. Many files are poorly organized, and they offer access to only a limited number of people. One solution may be a blending of microcomputer technology with existing micrographic techniques. The result: a computer-assisted retrieval system. This permits documents to be filmed and indexed at random. The computer keeps track of where the filmed material is located and directs readers to the right frame.

As automated offices become more common, we'll all be working a little smarter. Do whatever you can to keep aware of the advances being made in office technology, appraising how these new methods and machines can help you and your colleagues to obtain and process information and to communicate more effectively.

COPING WITH PAPER

If your office is like most offices, a great wave of paper—letters, memos, reports, contracts and trade newspapers and magazines—

crosses your desk each day. Unless you learn how to handle it, it can engulf you.

The paper problem keeps getting bigger and bigger Copy machines contribute to the glut as do computers. A fast-printing computer can print out enough paper to bury you in the time it takes you to read this paragraph. The federal government is another contributor. Both business and private institutions are deluged with forms and reports the government wants filled out.

Do whatever you can to shield yourself from the daily paper onslaught. Have your secretary or an assistant handle the routine sorting. Only paper that requires your attention should arrive at your desk. And you should only deal with each piece of paper once.

When it does arrive, stack it in a neat pile. Have a wastebasket close by. Pick up each item, scan it and decide what to do with it. With most people, all paper falls into one of five categories:

1. *Urgent.* These are items that demand your immediate attention. If a letter or memo brings a request for a decision, make the decision immediately (as long as you have all the facts). If a letter is required, dictate it. If a telephone call is needed, make it. Don't put off doing anything that's urgent.

2. *Read and save.* This is important material. Stack up paper in this category and put it in a file folder. Whenever you have a few minutes, start reading from the stack. This is the kind of material that you can read when traveling. If the stack gets too big, schedule reading time to cut it down to size. As each item is read, mark it for filing or for action by a subordinate.

3. *Read and discard.* This is material of secondary importance. Trade newspapers and magazines are usually in this category. It's material you'd like to read but may not be able to because of other demands on your time. If a week or two passes and you still haven't read something in this category, it's best to toss it out. It has undoubtedly lost whatever importance it once had.

4. *File*. Make a note on each item in this category, instructing your secretary or assistant as to where it is to be filed. If you don't want to write on a particular piece of paper, put your instructions on note paper and staple it to the item.

5. *Discard*. Most of your paper will go into the wastebasket. Robert Moskowitz says that one rough measure of how well you manage your time is how large a proportion of all incoming paper goes directly into the wastebasket.

"Try to handle each piece of paper only once" is one of Alan Lakein's rules for coping with the paper blitzkrieg. Once you pick up a piece of paper, don't put it down without doing something that advances the project the paper represents. "If you can't take a big step," says Lakein, "even the smallest step counts." Failing to act after picking up a piece of paper the first time means that at some future time you're going to have to pick it up again. That's not working smart.

Try this test: Whenever you pick up a piece of paper, put a tiny check mark in the lower right-hand corner. When the check marks begin to accumulate, it's a warning that you've wasted too much time on the subject, and it's about time you made a decision concerning it.

A TICKLER FILE

Each delivery of paper is likely to bring with it at least one request for you to take action on some matter at a later date. Let's say you get a memo from your boss, early in the month, asking for a breakdown on your department's budget by the end of the month. You know it's going to take you a couple of days to get the information together. A tickler file will remind you when to act. To set up such a file, you need one of those accordion-shaped file folders with individual compartments. Number the compartments from one to 31, corresponding to each day of the month. Put the boss's memo in the slot marked 23. That will give you a whole week to prepare the figures.

The last thing at night before you go home, go through the tickler for the next day. On the 23rd, you'll find the boss's memo. When you get the information together, put it and the memo in the compartment marked 30 or 31 (the last day of the month). Then you'll remember to give the boss the information on the date he or she wanted it.

Each morning when you are writing out your list of the things you want to accomplish during the day, make reference to the tickler file. Be sure to include the items that turn up in the slot for that day.

EXPERT ADVICE

As Denslow Brown points out earlier in this chapter, getting organized is very much an individual matter. An idea that works well for one person may be worthless for someone else. In the pages that follow, businessmen and writers, politicians and actors, disclose some of the widely varied methods they rely upon for greater achievement and better performance.

· · · · ·

J. Jeffrey Campbell

Chairman and chief executive officer, Burger King Corporation

I have several "secrets" for making efficient use of my business day. One thing I try to do is separate all the thinking work from the processing work. Right now on my desk I have two stacks of paper. One is all the strategic-thought, move-the-business-ahead stuff. The other is the trivial stuff you have to face in any business, mostly correspondence on less than high-priority issues.

There's some processing stuff I have to reply to myself. I can't delegate it; my secretary can't handle it with a form letter. That kind of stuff I just get out at random periods throughout the day—first thing in the morning or between meetings, time like that. Or sometimes I'll take it home. And I'll sit with a legal pad and watch a ball game, and on the commercial breaks I'll write a memo. And it's amazing, during a couple of periods of a football game I'll knock off fifteen or twenty memos.

The brainwork I do when I have a sizeable block of time in the office. Or I'll occasionally take an afternoon off and go home with it. It's quiet there, no telephones ringing. I can spend two, three, four hours concentrating.

Another time I do brainwork is early on Saturday or Sunday mornings. My wife gets up about 9 or 9:30. I tend to get up around 7 or 7:30. I've got two hours of work without bothering anybody. In the morning I find myself very fresh. My mind is clear as a bell. I can get a helluva lot done. Again, the phone's not ringing; there are no interruptions. I can knock off something in two hours on a Saturday morning that might take me days to do at the office.

The airplane is a great time to do brainwork. Almost any flight I take from Miami (where the company's headquarters is located) is two-and-one-half or three-and-one-half hours. I find flying terribly dull. So the airplane is the perfect place to sit and knock off a think piece, something that takes a little extra effort.

Another thing I do is have my secretary intercept a lot of the trivial mail, and I never see it. She sends some things on to other people. She takes the junk mail out. She pretty much knows the stuff I want to see and the stuff I don't want to see. I probably only get two-thirds of the stuff that comes in.

· · · · ·

Orrin G. Hatch
U.S. Senator (Utah)

Although I try to work smart, I certainly work hard. I have so many issues to deal with that the amount of paper generated with respect thereto can be almost unmanageable. I have, therefore, found it necessary to develop a system to conserve my time.

I require each of my legislative assistants to supply materials on current legislation on a "one-pager." The background, the issue itself, the arguments pro and con, analysis, alternative solutions, and a recommended decision must be clearly expressed on a single page. The bill itself and other background materials, as well as more extensive memoranda, may be attached as thought necessary; but I want one-page decision documents.

Each document is reviewed by my administrative assistant, who logs it in, and he determines its relative immediacy and sends it to me in that order. The bottom-line of each document is a predetermined decision format so that I need only check the alternative I choose and initial it. It moves immediately back to my administrative assistant, who logs it out and returns it to the appropriate legislative assistant for implementation.

·　·　·　·　·

Arthur Hailey
〰〰〰〰〰〰〰〰〰〰〰〰〰

Author, In High Places (Dell, 1986; first published 1961),
Airport (Dell, 1986; first published 1968), Strong Medicine
(Dell, 1986)

Dispose of paperwork either immediately, or as soon as possible after it comes in, then it doesn't accumulate and become a formidable pile. (Never have a "pending" tray—It's a procrastinator; crutch.) But don't read anything (example, mail) until you are ready to deal with it. Then handle it promptly, making needed decisions, and move on to whatever is next. However, be ruthless in refusing to give time to the irrelevant and unsolicited.

Schedule work in well-defined hours, leaving periods for leisure, and be firm in not allowing the leisure time to be eroded.

Be systematic always. The small time taken in personally developing a good filing and record system can save hours and hours afterward.

Above all, make up your mind if you're going to do something, do it. If you're not, having reached that decision, put it out of mind.

· · · · ·

Henry Ford II

Business executive

One point I offer is to underscore the importance of appearing at meetings fully prepared for discussion, debate and decision-making. That's accomplished by doing "homework"—reading the background papers and understanding the pros and cons of proposals and positions. I also suggest that there are occasions when there is no substitute for long hours, particularly when reviewing operations overseas or at locations which are not visited by a manager on a frequent basis.

· · · · ·

Gay Talese

Author, *Thy Neighbor's Wife* (Doubleday, 1980), *The Kingdom and the Power* (Dell, 1981), *Honor Thy Father* (Dell, 1981), *Fame and Obscurity* (Dell, 1984)

I've never thought "proper planning and organization" achieved anything in writing that did not involve finally, and totally, hard work of the most primitive type—which is *no* typewriter, no word processor, no tape recorder, nothing but a pen and pad and CONSTANT rewriting. The New Technology, I think, has made writing easier—and softer and more shallow. The tape recorder has definitely ruined the "ear" of young researchers, and you can always tell a tape-recorder book. People who think in terms of time-efficiency should not be writing books, but should be doing something else—making millions on Wall Street or designing shopping malls—but not struggling with the language and its refinement.

. . . . .

Stewart Mott
▲▲▲▲▲▲▲▲▲▲▲▲▲▲▲▲▲▲▲

Business executive, political activist

Use any scrap paper if letrhd not handy
Abbrev always
Write own ltrs & rarely
Skip lunch
Work at home—no commute
Shop by mail order
Avoid mtgs—use phone
Conf calls & spkfone—to speed decisions
Read/scan print-media—TV/Radio too linear
Listen subliminally to all-news radio
Hands-free phone: take notes, avoid neck-ache, do chores,
file nails, read
Bathe 3–4X/wk—daily = bore
Moped to mid-town appts
Delegate, delegate, delegate
Avoid "Hello, how are you?"—start conversation immed
Remember to look at the flowers
Eschew cute quotes for popular publ

. . . . .

Eli Wallach
▲▲▲▲▲▲▲▲▲▲▲▲▲▲▲▲▲▲▲

Actor

During my five year hitch in the U.S. Army, I was a Registrar &
Detachment Commander in Army hospitals—and there I learned
to never let correspondence pile up. A clean desk represented an
organized mind. In the theatre our time is managed for us—and
we must be disciplined enough to obey the dictates of theatre, TV
and film. The actor must be aware of curtain-time, air-time, and

reporting to the movie set on time. I have little patience with time-wasters or late comers. They add a burden to already complicated lives.

. . . . .

Susan K. Jones

Author (with W. Lauren R. Januz), *Time Management for Executives* (Scribner, 1982)

This is one of my favorites. Except for important client communications, reply to short requests by hand, right on the request. If necessary, keep a photo copy of the whole page for your files.

. . . . .

William L. Armstrong

U.S. Senator (Colorado)

Issues, people, letters and paperwork must all be dealt with on a case-by-case basis. There are a couple of rules I do try to apply, however. First, avoid handling the same piece of paper twice; make whatever decision is required, take the action indicated and move on. Second, make sure all meetings have a purpose. Many busy people spend a great deal of time in meetings, so it is important that such meetings have an agenda, whether written or not.

. . . . .

Arthur Miller

Playwright

I can tell you that my efforts to manage my time only succeed when I don't answer my mail.

. . . . .

J.P. Donlon

Editor, *Chief Executive*

As an amateur military historian, specializing in the Napoleonic age, let me pass along one timeless piece of time management practiced by the Emperor of the French as related by his private secretary, and schoolmate at Brienne, Louis Antoine Fauvelet de Bourrienne. During his campaigns Napoleon conducted the affairs of state wherever the Grand Army's headquarters were pitched. Letters requiring his attention and numerous petitions piled up unopened. Napoleon's system was to answer only those documents requiring immediate attention. The passage of time, he reasoned, would obviate the need for his intervention for the rest.

. . . . .

Reggie Jackson

Professional baseball player; real estate investor

Delegate. Delegate. I delegate everything. I try to find quality people, and they I pay them well. It's better to overpay good people than underpay poor people. Good people will perform for you. They'll do 12 hours of work in an eight-hour day. They'll do things for you that you won't even know about. A good insurance man won't just buy whatever policy happens to be available; he'll go out and look for a good deal. A good secretary won't spend time on the telephone with her friends, or try to stretch her lunch hour. She'll question bills that come in. When she runs an errand for you, she'll take a bus instead of a cab if it's just as convenient. When she makes a purchase for you, she'll shop around. I couldn't operate without good help.

. . . . .

Susan Brownmiller

Author, *Against Our Will; Men, Women and Rape* (Simon & Schuster, 1975), *Femininity* (Linden Press, 1984)

Instant coffee in the morning and leave the bed unmade. Attend to business mail once a month. Refuse all speaking engagements, and—a new one for me—ignore all requests to write blurbs for other writers' books. To be honest, time squandering is my true specialty. A one-hour bath in the morning is my best creative-thinking time. I am lucky to live with a man who enjoys the food-gathering aspects of life and who can't go to sleep in an unmade bed. I find that he saves me a lot of time, among other things. The dog and the garden are tremendously inefficient in terms of time management, but I have compensated a little by cutting out the phone answering service. No need to call anyone back!

5

Controlling Job Stress

Your palms sweat before a crucial meeting. You get persistent headaches when you have to work fast or under pressure.

Your back, neck and shoulder muscles feel tight and sore at the end of a frantic day. You have stomach pains or digestive problems at the end of a tough week.

You feel exhausted yet you have trouble sleeping.

You're beginning to experience periods of irritability, anger or depression.

Everyone who works is touched by job stress. It's more common than ringing telephones and morning traffic jams. Coping strategies include hurrying one's lunch, biting one's nails, getting up late, taking days off, compulsive eating, smoking and drinking.

And drug taking. It is a sign of the stressful times that the best selling drugs in the country are an ulcer medication (Tagamet), a hypertension drug (Inderal) and a tranquilizer (Valium).

Job-related stress causes inefficiency and lowers productiveness. It can also be dangerous to your health. Indeed, the chronic stress induced by the demands of the workplace has come to be recognized as one of the most serious health hazards of the day. Medical problems associated with job stress include high blood pressure, gastritis, ulcers, colitis and heart disease, plus obesity and alcoholism. The American Institute of Stress says that 70 to 90 percent of all visits to physicians are triggered by stress-related disorders.

Over the long run, job stress can lead to burnout. The early symptoms are exhaustion, physical illness, acute anger and depression. In later stages, the illness can become incapacitating; there is deep pessimism and self-doubt. Ultimately, burnout can be life threatening.

Leaders in business and industry have become alarmed at the escalating costs of stress, which are evidenced by absenteeism, lost productivity and burgeoning company medical expenses. Costs to industry are estimated at $150 billion annually, says the American Institute of Stress. Stress-related workers' compensation awards threaten to bankrupt the system in some states.

About one in five of the *Fortune* 500 companies now offers at least one of several stress-management programs. These can range from alcoholism programs, which are the most common, to exercise facilities and meditation classes. New York Telephone Co., for example, requires periodic health examinations for all employees and offers meditation training for those with stress-related problems. These programs are said to have cut the corporate hypertension rate from 18%, which is about average, to half that amount. New York Telephone says that it is saving about $130,000 a year in reduced absenteeism.

Even if your company offers no stress reduction programs, you can take the matter into your own hands. It's important to realize that you can't escape stress. It's a part of virtually every work situation, and it increases when the pressures of your job increase, pressures brought on by such things as a tough deadline or a boss who yells.

Though you can't escape job stress, you can learn to cope with it. The first step is to spot stress in its early stages. Frequent headaches or a churning stomach are indications that your stress level is high. Once you're aware of stress, it's time to do something to get it under control. Maybe you have to rethink your goals or reorganize your work schedule. Maybe you can help yourself by eating more healthful foods or exercising regularly.

This chapter identifies the men and women most likely to suffer from job-related stress and examines what they can do to combat it.

THE POWER CONNECTION

The greatest stress occurs in jobs where the individual faces heavy psychological demands, yet has little control over how to get the work done. It's a case of too much work, too little clout. As this may suggest, workers who feel stress the most are often those in middle management. They face the pressures of making their way up the corporate ladder, but they must also shoulder a heavy responsibility—and still must answer to superiors who have ultimate say over the work.

Those who have made their way to the top have the fewest problems. They, of course, have a good deal of control over how they do their jobs; they are in charge of the work process. In addition, they have the opportunity to develop new skills in their work, to grow, which helps them increase their self-confidence.

Money does not play a vital role. That is, individuals in better paying jobs are about as likely to suffer stress as those with modest salaries. Sure, a higher-than-average income can make life easier and more secure, which tends to reduce some of the pressures of family life. But money alone is not nearly as important as the demands made upon the individual and the methods used to meet those demands.

These are not the only factors. Certain events intensify stress. Specialists in this field agree that the most stressful event of all is getting fired. Any drastic change can trigger stress. Anytime you begin a new job, switch careers, or even change the amount or kind of responsibility you have, expect increased stress. Trouble with your boss or a coworker or a change in work hours or conditions will boost your stress level, too.

STRESS AND DISTRESS

In his book, *Stress Without Distress,* Hans Selye, M.D., the Canadian endocrinologist who became widely known for his pioneering studies concerning the body's physiological response to stress, explains that the word "stress," like the words "success," "failure" and "happiness," means different things to different people. Defining stress is no easy matter, he says.

To Selye, stress is "the nonspecific response of the body to any demand made upon it." By nonspecific, Selye means a response that affects all parts of a system, not merely a few units of it. Step outdoors on a day when the temperature is in the 90s, and your body starts sweating. When exposed to freezing cold your body shivers. Heat and cold thus cause stress. So does a game of chess or a passionate embrace, says Selye.

"Even when fully relaxed and asleep, you are under some stress," Selye declares. "Your heart must continue to pump blood, your intestines to digest, and your muscles to move your chest for respiration."

None of these, Selye points out, cause any harmful effects. Damaging or unpleasant stress he calls *dis*tress.

What Selye is saying is that stress is not something that you should avoid. The truth is, you couldn't if you wanted to.

" 'Stress' is a physiological concept that describes certain degrees of tension load on the neurological system," says Dr. John M. Phelan, director of the Communications Research Institute at New York's Fordham University. "In this sense it is neutral. Jogging, tennis, chess, sex and touring are all pleasantly stressful—'stimulating,' 'toning.'

"Toothaches, anxiety, anger, terror, depression, just simple impatience are unpleasantly stressful. If a mere diagnostic machine measured heart rate, blood pressure, peristalsis and other signs of stress of the same healthy twenty-year-old when about to make love or make war, the readings might be identical. But the *experience,* the interpretation of the stress based on knowledge of the cause, would be worlds apart. I have had sleepless nights of worry and of great happiness."

Stress is "the spice of life," Selye says, declaring " . . . we can meet it efficiently and enjoy it . . . by learning more about its mechanism and adjusting our life accordingly."

THE A MAN

He always plays to win, even in a game with children.
He often tries to do two things at once.
He hurries or interrupts the speech of others.
He gets irritated if kept waiting for any reason.
He makes a fetish of always being on time.
He distrusts other peoples' motives.
He talks with his hands or pounds his fist for emphasis.
He often jiggles a knee or taps his fingers.
He has trouble sitting and doing nothing.

These are some of the characteristics of what has been classified as Type A behavior. The term began to be heard in the 1960s when a pair of cardiologists from Mount Zion Medical Center in San Francisco, Dr. Meyer Friedman and Dr. Ray Rosenmann, first described the Type A personality, and declared that men with this behavior pattern seemed to be seven times more likely than others to have cardiac heart disease.

Friedman and Rosenmann contrasted the hostile and compulsive Type A, embodied by the tough, competitive male executive, determined beyond all reason to get to the top and stay there, with the Type B male, whom they characterized as being calmer and more relaxed. Their book, *Type A Behavior and Your Heart,* was published in 1974.

Although there is widespread acceptance of the idea that Type A behavior is an important factor in heart disease, many heart experts have expressed skepticism about the Friedman-Rosenmann findings. Personality and behavior, the skeptics say, are less important than such major risk factors as smoking, high blood pressure, high blood cholesterol and diabetes. The American Heart Association policy statement concerning the risk factors for coronary heart disease recognizes that Type A behavior increases cardiac risk but ranks it as a secondary factor.

Despite the questions that were raised, Dr. Friedman expanded upon his original research. In 1984, he announced the results of a three-year federally funded study of more than 800 men who had suffered heart attacks. The study demonstrated that counseling to reduce the characteristics of Type A behavior could cut in half the chances of suffering a second heart attack. "If changing behavior can have such a striking effect on people with well-established heart disease," said Dr. Friedman, "it should be even more helpful to those who have not yet had a heart attack."

The study, conducted by a team from Mount Zion Hospital and Medical Center and Stanford University School of Education in Palo Alto, involved 862 volunteers who were randomly assigned to either a "treatment" or "control" group. Twice as many men were assigned to the treatment group as to the control group because it was expected that the dropout rate would be much higher among those undergoing behavior modification. "Type A people," Dr. Friedman explained, "often have a hard time recognizing their self-destructive behavior and an even harder time deciding to change it." They have no patience for dealing with such matters, he added.

During the course of the study, the participants had 44 counseling sessions with trained therapists over the three-year period. The men were instructed to make lists of their activities, and were then urged to consider giving up those that they performed for the sake of their egos, rather than for love or necessity.

They were taught new habits to replace those identified with Type A conduct. They were taught, for example, how to smile openly and often. They were given daily drills with such instructions as: "Do something nice and unpredictable for your spouse," "Smile at people in the street," "Take 15 minutes alone and do nothing except listen to music," and "Listen to someone talk without thinking about something else and saying anything until they are done."

Other drills included "Look at yourself in the mirror at midday and again after work to see if your face shows any signs of irritation or anger," "Play a game and plan to lose," "Laugh at yourself" and "Avoid other angry Type As."

After the three years of psychological guidance, 9% of the men had recurrent heart attacks. But this figure stood in sharp contrast to the 19% heart attack rate among men in the control group who were given only standard cardiological advice about diet, exercise and therapies.

As these findings seem to suggest, serious stress problems can be eased through professionally-directed behavior modification. If you are interested in such a program, ask your doctor for a referral to a therapist or counselor with training in stress management as well as psychotherapy. Since this is a relatively new field, there may not be a practitioner in your area. There are, however, new stress-reduction clinics opening all the time, many of them affiliated with leading hospitals or medical centers.

The American Institute of Stress (124 Park Ave., Yonkers, NY 10703) can also be helpful. A not-for-profit organization founded in 1978, the AIS offers a comprehensive list of stress-reduction services available throughout the country and, when feasible, an evaluation of such efforts.

E WOMEN

During 1984, Harriet B. Braiker, PhD, a clinical psychologist in private practice in Los Angeles, and a director of a training group specializing in corporate stress management programs for women, identified the Type E woman. Unlike the single-minded Type A male with his compulsion for professional success, the Type E woman pushes herself to be *Everything* to *Everybody*. She strives to succeed in her varied and multiple roles—at home, at work and in the community. She is pulled in several directions at once. Stress and stress-related illness are the result.

"Underlying the personality of the Type E woman," said Dr. Braiker in an article in *Working Woman,* "is a marked sense of insecurity and a desperate striving to convince herself that she is worthwhile, important and competent."

What is the solution? What can the Type E woman do to conquer the stress in her life? One thing that Dr. Braiker recommends is "quieting" breaks. Five minutes before a meeting or phone call that is perceived to be stressful, close your office door, close your eyes and breathe deeply and rhythmically while visualizing yourself lying on a warm beach listening to the ocean. Try to feel completely relaxed.

Delegation and negotiation are other ways to cope. In delegating, "Don't apologize," says Dr. Braiker. "Too often," she states, "Type E women feel compelled to explain why they are not able to do everything themselves—as if they *should*."

Negotiation involves discussing demands made upon your time. When asked to do something by her boss or a family member, the Type-E woman responds as if the request were an ultimatum. She offers no input into the way the demand is structured. There is no give and take. "Requests—and even responsibilities—are negotiable," says Dr. Braiker. "When necessary, try bargaining for time."

The important thing is to remain in control. When things pile up and a breaking point seems just over the horizon, take a few minutes to make a list of all the alternatives you have, even though some of them may seem unrealistic or unpalatable. Then, after assessing the advantages and disadvantages of each, choose the best route. You'll be heartened by the fact that it's *your* decision, not one that's being forced upon you.

But the "real cure" for the Type-E woman, says Dr. Braiker, "lies in altering her relationship with herself." She has to come to an understanding that her right to happiness is hers uncondition-ally. It is not linked to the false notion that she can *have it all* only by *doing it all*.

LEARNING TO RELAX

Techniques such as muscle relaxation, rhythmic breathing and bio-feedback (in which an attempt is made to consciously regulate heartbeat or blood pressure) have gained wide acceptance in help-ing victims control stress. It's a good idea to take 10 or 20 minutes once or twice a day to practice one of these techniques that works for you. The result can be a significant and lasting reduction of stress-related symptoms.

On-the-Job Relaxation. When things seem to be getting out of hand, take a few minutes and try to totally relax, physically and mentally. Close your eyes, take three deep breaths, and as you exhale let each part of your body go limp—from your forehead, your eyes, nose, chin, neck, shoulders, and all the way down. When you reach your toes, picture a very relaxing scene: a calm lake, a stream with a magnificent mountain view, an empty ocean beach or maybe a steaming hot bath. Visualize every detail of the scene. Imagine how warm you feel, the sounds you hear. Empty your mind of all other thoughts.

Focus on those areas of your body that are most affected by stress. Tighten these muscles as hard as you can, and hold them tight for about 15 seconds, then relax them. At the same time, exhale deeply. Feel the relaxation ripple through your body.

Meditation. Meditation, in general, and Transcendental Medi-tation (TM), in particular, have also proven successful in relaxing stress-wracked bodies. TM, which was introduced to the United

States in the late 1950s by Maharishi Mahesh Yogi, a Hindu monk from India, is a heightened state of consciousness that combines extreme mental alertness and deep physical repose. Practitioners say that TM enables them to think more clearly and that their thoughts are more creative. It also causes them to feel rested.

People practice TM by sitting in a comfortable position with their eyes closed. They then silently repeat their mantra, a pleasant-sounding word from Hindu scriptures. They meditate for 15 to 20 minutes in the morning and evening, before meals.

Scientific studies have shown that TM can produce dramatic physiological changes. Blood pressure and the rate of heartbeat fall during meditation. Alpha waves—brain waves that become prominent when a person is relaxed—increase during meditation. TM is a natural antidote to tension.

"I'm a fairly high strung and anxious person; TM has been invaluable to me," says Donna Brooks, a senior editor of children's books, at E.P. Dutton. "When I started meditation I couldn't believe that I had survived without it. It calmed me down. It took away a certain kind of nervous, vibratory quality I have. You still have to face whatever you have to face when you're done meditating, but you feel so much better that you make better decisions. You're more creative, more energetic.

"I learned TM the way anyone learns it, from an instructor, someone who was properly qualified. And I just sit and follow the instructions twice a day for twenty minutes—in the morning preferably before breakfast, and again at the end of the day, preferably before dinner.

"You can meditate anywhere. You don't have to meditate where it's extremely quiet; you can meditate on the subway, although it's not as pleasurable. Sometimes I meditate in the office. Say I'm going to the ballet or some other event after work; then I meditate in my office at the end of the day. But if I'm just going home in the evening, then I would prefer to meditate there.

"The point of TM is that it's a preparation for activity. And that's why it's so useful to a person who is working hard and has to be flexible during the day, a person who deals with a lot of people and has to make important decisions. TM allows the mind to settle down completely, naturally; it allows the mind to take its own course. And when you become active again, you bring some of that restful alertness into your activity. You bring greater perspicacity, more brightness, quicker reflexes.

"I wouldn't conduct my life without TM. It's made me less harried. I still get harried. But TM is like a good night's sleep. You'll be less harried than if you had a poor night's sleep."

Some 300 centers that teach TM operate throughout the United States and Canada. For the address of a center in your area, consult the white pages of your telephone directory under the heading "Transcendental Meditation." Each center offers a seven-step introductory course of lectures, interviews, personal instruction and "verification and validation" experiences.

Two worthwhile books on the subject are: *Management of Stress; Using TM at Work,* by David R. Frew (Nelson-Hall, 1977) and *The TM Technique: A Skeptic's Guide to the TM Program,* by Peter Russell (Routledge & Kegan, 1977).

BIOFEEDBACK

An ever-increasing number of men and women with high-pressure jobs are using biofeedback to control the stress in their lives. They've learned to will away such stress symptoms as insomnia, muscle tension and even high blood pressure.

Biofeedback, a word coined by Barbara B. Brown, a California psychologist, is a technique for controlling bodily functions that were once thought to be completely involuntary—heart rate, brain waves, muscle tension and perspiration. You learn the technique at a hospital or clinic. The person in charge connects you by sensor wires to a machine with a televisionlike screen that feeds back information on such stress indicators as blood pressure, facial muscle tension and the temperature of the fingers (the colder, the tenser). By loosening your muscles, breathing deeply and letting your thoughts drift, you can be taught to control stress responses. Some patients make their blood pressure drop and increase the temperature of their fingers by as much as 14 degrees. Patients ultimately learn to produce the relaxation responses at home without the aid of the machines.

Biofeedback should not be confused with meditation or relaxation techniques (see above). While these can be helpful to some, they're seldom successful in healing stress-related symptoms—such as migraine headache or Reynaud's disease—that are already locked into the nervous system. Clinical biofeedback techniques, on the other hand, are now widely used to treat tension headaches, migraine headaches, disorders of the digestive system, high blood pressure and its opposite, low blood pressure, and Reynaud's disease.

Biofeedback machines include the electromyograph (or EMG, for measuring muscle tension), the electroencephalograph (or EEG, for measuring brain waves), the galvanic skin response (or GSR, which measures sweat) and the thermistor, that keeps track of body temperature. Most people require 15 to 25 sessions on the machines to determine the relaxation technique that works best for them. The best results are obtained when treatment is begun as soon as possible after the symptoms develop. The price is usually around $100 per session.

Patients are also encouraged to examine and perhaps modify their habit patterns. "We suggest they examine their time demands, perfectionist tendencies and overreaction to key persons in their lives," says Dr. Keith W. Sedlacek, director of the Stress Regulation Institute in New York City, writing in *Consultant* magazine. "We suggest they create a healthier environment for themselves."

Some patients begin to acquire skill in relaxing within the first few sessions. They report feeling relaxed, "heavy" or "floating." They are able to let their minds drift.

For more information on biofeedback, inquire at your local medical center or university. Or write the Biofeedback Society of America (4301 Owens St., Wheat Ridge, CO 80003). The organization publishes a directory that lists individual practitioners and the stress-related problems treated by each.

EATING RIGHT

Certain foods can help you cope with stress, while others are detrimental, slowing you down and contributing to your nervousness. Whole grain products that don't contain sugar, salt or fat are your best bet. Among those that you can bring to the office are whole wheat bread or bread sticks, whole grain crackers, rice cakes and whole grain cereals—Grape Nuts, shredded wheat, Nutrigrain or puffed rice, puffed wheat or puffed corn.

Foods with a high fat content (such as cheese, whole milk, yogurt, nuts, seeds, eggs and processed meats) can make you feel sluggish unless eaten with other foods.

Keep away from caffeine. Too much can make you jittery and irritable. It makes you prone to headaches, too. Coffee, tea, cola drinks and chocolate contain caffeine.

Avoid foods with simple carbohydrates. They make your blood sugar rise and fall too quickly, which brings on fatigue. Skip candy, cake, cookies, soft drinks and other foods with an obviously high sugar content.

Salty snacks should also be avoided. Salt makes you feel bloated because it encourages your body to retain water. Potato chips, corn chips, pretzels and such are among the salt-laden snack foods.

Many people seek to cope with a heavy workload by skipping the midday meal entirely or grabbing a sandwich and a diet soda, or a cup of yogurt and a candy bar at their desk. No matter how you happen to view this practice, it's wrong.

In the first place, it does nothing to reduce stress. You may get a bit more work out but you're paying a very high price. You need a midday break. You need to change your environment, leave your desk and the stale office air behind and seek some privacy. This doesn't necessarily mean that you have to go off by yourself somewhere. A busy city street can provide a stimulating change.

Some people justify a skimpy lunch by telling themselves that it's beneficial from a weight reduction standpoint. That argument doesn't hold water, either. Nutritionists say that it's better to eat the main meal of the day at lunchtime, and a light meal in the evening.

Skipping lunch is also a mistake physiologically. When you go without lunch, your energy level is likely to nosedive during the afternoon. Then, when fatigue and hunger strike, you reach for whatever is close at hand—coffee, a soft drink, a candy bar from a vending machine, or a similar snack from an office coffee wagon. The combination of sugar, salt and fats serves to exacerbate your energy problem.

The best kind of lunch for people in a hurry and under stress is one that offers a balanced combination of about one-third protein and two-thirds carbohydrates. The protein can be provided by a cup of yogurt, a glass of milk, a hard-boiled egg, or lean meat (turkey and chicken are the best) or cheese in a sandwich made from wheat or other whole grain bread. A tuna fish sandwich, a lean-meat hamburger or a serving of fish with a baked potato gets very high marks.

Company cafeterias, some fast-food outlets and big-city green-grocers now offer salad bars. Salad for lunch is fine. But be selective. Choose fresh, raw vegetables. Combine them with a hard-boiled egg or cube of tofu for protein. Avoid the commercial salad dressing, laden with too much oil, salt and sugar. Substitute a sprinkling of lemon or wine vinegar or a spoonful of vegetable oil.

You should not only eat well during periods of stress, but also drink well. "People under prolonged emotional stress should drink plenty of fluids," says Brian L.G. Morgan, assistant professor of nutrition at Columbia University's Institute of Human Nutrition, in New York City. Writing in *RX Being Well,* he explains that during times of anxiety the body may act to conserve fluids and salts. Drinking more encourages the body to excrete the excess fluids. Professor Morgan says that it is also a good idea to consume more potassium-rich foods, such as bananas, apricots, potatoes, spinach, chicken, milk and orange juice. They can help to alleviate symptoms of migraine headache.

Other nutrients that are likely to be depleted during periods of stress are B vitamins (found in cereals, vegetables and meats) and vitamin C (found in citrus fruits, tomatoes, cabbage and potatoes).

Should you take special formulations to compensate for the loss? Such supplements, frequently termed "stress vitamins," typically provide megadoses of C and B vitamins (but none of the others needed to meet the Recommended Daily Allowances). Since these can be expensive, a better solution is probably a vitamin/mineral supplement with a balanced assortment of nutrients comparable to the RDAs.

OTHER COPING STRATEGIES

Much of the research into stress and preventive medicine has focused on what psychologists call "hardiness" or a coping personality. A number of factors seem to be helpful in adopting such behavior. These include a sense of being in control of one's life and having friends and family available to provide social support. Such personality characteristics as flexibility and hopefulness are important.

Here are some techniques you can employ in seeking to keep stress under control.

Have Realistic Goals. The search for perfection is often singled out as the No. 1 cause of stress. Perfection, says the dictionary, is the highest degree of proficiency, skill or excellence—and it's unattainable. Don't strive for perfection. Don't struggle to attain impractical, unrealizable goals. Do so and you'll wind up frustrated; it's self-imposed stress.

The solution may be to reevaluate your goals. Ask yourself whether your job, and the duties you perform, is giving you the chance to achieve your goals. Would you prefer to perform different functions, have different responsibilities? Should you consider changing jobs completely?

Set Priorities. Budget your time and energy. What are the most important things to do today? Make a list. If there are six things on the list, start with the most important items. "Do those first," says Dr. Donald Tubesing, author of *Kicking Your Stress Habit.* "Then, if you still have time, move on to the least important items. Scattering your energies is not only bad for your nerves," he warns, "it also affects the quality of your work." (For more on making lists and setting priorities, see Chapter 2, pp. 55–57.)

Learn to pace yourself; work steadily. What you don't want to do is work in sudden bursts of frantic energy. That's highly stressful.

Get to know your body clock. What time of the day do you operate the best? When does your body begin to slow down? (See Chapter 3, "Prime Time," pp. 85–88.)

Stop Procrastinating. Don't postpone until tomorrow what you can do today, especially if the work involved is difficult or unpleasant. (Procrastination, its causes and cures, is the subject of Chapter 6.) The "secret" of overcoming procrastination is not to try to accomplish everything all at once; chip away at the project bit by bit. It's likely the task will get completed sooner than you think.

Dealing with Your Boss. Let's say your boss is the No. 1 stress producer in your life. He or she calls you at home almost every weekend and routinely keeps you at the office until nine or ten at night. You have to try to handle this problem in a direct manner. Explain to your boss that you approach your work differently, that you're able to accomplish what you want to accomplish by working a normal schedule. Tell your boss that you value your personal life.

Will this solve the problem? Probably not. You certainly shouldn't expect such an explanation to do much toward advancing your career. Your boss may tell you that he or she respects your position. But if the boss is a confirmed workaholic, he or she will probably expect you to continue to toil evenings and weekends in the same manner that he or she toils. H. Michael Hayes, a professor of business at the University of Colorado, in an interview in *Fortune* magazine, admitted that he was a workaholic in the years he had spent at General Electric. He was asked whether it bothered him when his subordinates failed to put in the same long hours as he did. "Yes," he admitted. "I'd think, 'What's the matter? They're not interested in the job.' "

A certified workaholic in a high position undoubtedly produces stress in the workplace as a whole. Perhaps you can enlist the support of your coworkers in getting changes made. Working with other employees, draw up a list of what should be done to moderate job stress. Perhaps you're seeking increased control over your workload, a greater part in decision-making, or opportunities to learn more skills. Bring these suggestions to the boss in a nonconfrontational manner.

You may not get a positive response right away; indeed, the chances are very good you won't. But at least you and your coworkers have opened up the issue of stress for discussion, and by banding together you've increased the likelihood that change will be instituted at some future date.

Don't Let Anger Sit Inside. It's sometimes better to fight back than take abuse. Expressing anger can clear the air and relieve a lot of pressure. But don't get angry over trivial matters; be sure it's an issue worth fighting for.

Talk Out Your Problem. The worst problems are those you keep to yourself. Discussing a job-related problem with a trusted friend or counselor often leads to a solution. For example, you may not be able to shout back to your boss but you can get things off your chest by talking to a coworker. He or she is probably angry at the same things you are, and together you may think of ways to solve some of the problems. At the very least, the discussion will lighten the burden.

Mentally Divorce Yourself from Troubling Situations. A salesman for a chain of hardware stores was constantly being berated by customers for late deliveries of ordered merchandise. "I finally realized that these people weren't yelling at me—they were yelling at the company," he says. Once he was able to convince himself not to take the remarks personally, he stopped simmering inside.

Organize Your Personal Space. After a day spent in surroundings over which you have no control—the office, school, commuter trains, or busy streets or highways—you need to retreat to a private space that offers serenity, a refuge. Organize your living room, bedroom and study so they contribute to your tranquility. Get rid of clutter—stacks of newspapers and magazines, clothes you haven't worn for a year, appliances that work fitfully. Your home environment should stress comfort and convenience. Organize your drawers and closets; you should never have to search for anything. Put in some comfortable chairs and good reading lamps. Hang photographs and pictures that give you a warm feeling.

Take Time Out for Exercise. According to the *New England Journal of Medicine,* an exercise break in the middle of the day keeps one mentally sharp for four or five hours. It also serves as a safety valve, a method of unwinding. Thirty-five of the top 50 companies on the *Fortune* 500 list have fitness facilities for employees, and it's predicted that by 1990 10% of all U.S. corporations will offer fitness centers. If your firm doesn't have a gym or fitness center, and it's not convenient for you to whack a tennis ball or jog for half an hour or so, take a brisk walk around the block. Besides the physical benefits, exercise gets your mind off of your anxieties.

Make Time for Leisure. You owe it to yourself to take periodic vacations. Without time off, you risk burnout. (See Chapter 8.)

STRESS RESOURCES

For a rundown on a wide range of materials concerning stress management and "wellness promotion," including handbooks, workbooks, workshops and cassette tapes, write: Whole Person Associates, 1702 East Jefferson St., Duluth, MN 55812.

For a listing of reprints available on a variety of stress-related topics—"Occupational Stress," "Office Stress," "Physiology of Stress," "Stress and Arthritis," Stress and Families," etc.—send a stamped, self-addressed envelope to The American Institute of Stress, 124 Park Ave., Yonkers, NY 10703.

For a discussion of stress as an occupational hazard, see the report titled "Warning: Health Hazards for Office Workers," available from the Working Women Education Fund, 1224 Huron Rd., Cleveland, OH 44115; $6.50 for individuals; $10 for institutions, plus 80 cents postage.

. . . . .

Additional Reading
〰〰〰〰〰〰〰〰〰〰〰〰〰〰〰〰〰

The Stress of Life, by Hans Selye, MD (McGraw-Hill, 1956). The pioneering study. Some parts are highly technical.

Stress Without Distress, by Hans Selye, MD (Signet, 1974). How to use stress as a positive force in achieving a satisfying lifestyle.

Kicking Your Stress Habit, by Donald A. Tubesing, PhD (Signet, 1981). A do-it-yourself handbook for getting rid of unhealthy stress.

Stress, Sanity & Survival, by Robert L. Woolfolk, PhD, and Frank C. Richardson, PhD (Signet, 1978). The causes of stress and what to do about them.

Stress Management, by Edward Charlesworth, PhD, and Ronald G. Nathan, PhD (Ballantine, 1982). Techniques for dealing with stress at work, at home and in other areas of your life.

Burn-Out; The High Cost of High Achievement, by Herbert J. Freudenberger, PhD (Bantam, 1981). How to combat and cure the superachievers sickness.

The Type E Woman; How to Overcome the Stress of Being Everything to Everybody, by Harriet B. Braiker, PhD (Dodd, Mead, 1986). Coping skills to manage the multifarious demands that threaten to overwhelm the high-achieving woman.

Treating Type-A Behavior—And Your Heart, by Dr. Meyer Friedman and Diane Ulmer (Knopf, 1984). The findings of the study directed by Dr. Friedman, plus self-help tips.

EXPERT ADVICE

How can stress be prevented? According to Dr. John M. Ivancevich and Dr. Michael Matteson, both management professors at the University of Houston, companies can at least ease the problem by redesigning jobs, offering incentive rewards, identifying promotion possibilities more clearly, establishing preventative health practices and offering a variety of programs—from diet, nutrition and exercise plans to assertiveness training.

There are also many things that you yourself can do. Some tactics are more effective than others. Going to Bermuda for a few days is a good way to unwind after a tough week—but few can manage that. Drinking and medication may be easy ways of tuning out stress, but both present health hazards. Blowing off steam is usually merely a temporary solution. But there are many other methods of alleviating job stress, methods that are both practical and practicable. On the pages that follow, successful people ranging from Senator Strom Thurmond to weatherman Willard Scott share their techniques for coping with stress. These techniques can be as straightforward as playing a round of golf, getting a massage, or listening to music. The important thing is that they work for the "experts"—obviously the crucial factor for you in choosing a technique to control your stress.

· · · · ·

Jack Valenti
~~~~~~~~~~~~~~~~~~~~
President and chief executive officer, Motion Picture Association of America, Inc.

I have two methods for dealing with stress.

First, I remind myself that stress is transitory. It will pass. It always does. So while it is at fever pitch right now, it will subside in time, for that is always what happens. It is that foreknowledge that allows me to move through stress without it absorbing me, diminishing me.

Second, I always confront whatever issue is causing the stress. I don't wait and wonder and hope it will go away. I attack it. The mere fact of "doing something," of moving swiftly to challenge whatever it is that stirs the moment helps ease the pressure. Pressure and stress are most fierce when one is passive. Pressures fade when you move against them at their most strongly "defended" pressure point.

. . . . .

Liz Smith

Columnist; television commentator; author, *The Mother Book*; A *Compendium of Trivia and Grandeur Concerning Mothers, Motherhood and Maternity* (Crown, 1984)

Here's how I cope with stress:

I scream and yell a lot and never say "please" or "thank you" and everybody who works with me is understanding and pays no attention to me. Having to be polite in this job would kill me.

I have a massage twice a week which is the best answer for stress. And as my masseur is a young, handsome actor named Gary Tacon, that is a double whammy because I love him and he loves me and he makes me feel good.

I try to stay home occasionally at night, not answer the telephone, watch TV, eat crackers in bed, read a book, and answer the accumulated mail and junk. Getting it out of the way occasionally relieves stress. It is not possible for me to cope with mail and requests and so forth *on a daily basis.*

When I go out for fun, I go someplace like The Pink Tea Cup for lunch because it is friendly and hunkered down and not chic. That is a relief. In other words, try to do something different.

I sometimes lie down on a heating pad that makes moist heat. Just 10 minutes after a tough day at the typewriter relaxes my shoulders and neck and I am ready to go again.

Break for lunch, get on the old rowing machine, take a short nap, stop and call my mother in Texas—these are all stress reducers for me.

TEAR THE PHONE OUT OF THE WALL!

. . . . .

Kathy Keeton

President, *Omni* magazine; author, *Woman of Tomorrow* (St. Martin's, 1985)

The single best method for me to deal with tension and stress is regular exercise. Exercise lifts my spirits and gives me the energy I need to get back to a hectic schedule. As a result of a childhood battle against polio, I turned to ballet for therapy. I later earned a scholarship at the Sadler Wells Ballet School (The Royal Ballet) in London, and ballet has been a part of my life since.

As a dancer, I took my body seriously long before fitness became fashionable, and I still try to get to ballet class at least three or four times per week. Also to stay fit, and thus keep tension and stress at bay, I try to walk instead of ride, and to use stairs instead of elevators. In addition to exercise, research shows that a reduction of lifestyle risks such as aggression, high-fat diets, and over-indulgences will greatly enhance your body's ability to deal effectively with stress.

· · · · ·

John M. Phelan, PhD
^^^

Director, Communications Research Institute, and professor of communications, Fordham University; author, *Mediaworld*; *Programming the Public* (Continuum, 1977), *Disenchantment: Meaning & Morality in the Media* (Hastings House, 1980)

What to do about stress? First, do not see it as to be avoided in itself. Stress keeps us mentally and physically fit. Second, maintain a healthy life style as far as you can, so that your body can endure excessive stress and profit from normal stress. Third, know yourself; your moral character, your personal relationships, your professional status should be examined with pitiless honesty. In this way, one can pinpoint the real, as opposed to the imagined or wished-for, source of unpleasant stress. Fourth, deal with the causes of stress more than the symptoms. Decide and do! Don't delay or evade.

After all of this, there remain sources of unpleasant stress that we can of course neither avoid nor conquer: death, intractable pain, betrayal, the tragic sense of life. It would be fatuous to try to deal with these human conditions as if they were manageable minor ailments. Here we must more fundamentally turn to the moral order again: to faith, to hope, to love. We must truly believe what we tell our shivering children: Be brave, be strong.

Above all, be honest. The truth does set us free.

. . . . .

Strom Thurmond

U.S. Senator (South Carolina)

I find that exercising twice daily helps to alleviate the stress I face at work each day. My routine consists of situps, pushups, calisthenics, riding a stationary bicycle and swimming at least a mile or two each week. In addition, I abstain from caffeine, and too much sugar and fat in my diet. I also take vitamin supplements each day. A healthy individual can handle stress much easier than an unhealthy one.

When I make a decision, I do the best I can and then put it behind me. Worry is a great enemy, especially when you can do nothing more than you have already done.

. . . . .

John Fanning

Chairman of the board and president, Uniforce Temporary Personnel, Inc.; author, Work When You Want to Work (Pocket Books, 1985)

Do I feel stress? Not really. Sure, I get annoyed occasionally but it's seldom I feel any deep-seated anxiety. I was given some advice about thirty years ago and that's helped me avoid stress. I was going to give an address before the American Chemical Society. I was nineteen years old. Although I had had some experience in debating in college, I had never spoken before such a prestigious group. The speech was very important to me; a great deal was on the line. I was extremely apprehensive as the time drew near. Just as I was about to go on, a friend of mine said to me, "John, think about this—a hundred years from now no one is going to remember your speech." That was like the word from above to me. I realized I was not involved in some earth-shattering experience. What the hell, I thought to myself, it's not *that* important. And I went out and gave what was probably the best talk of my life. Ever since, that advice has been an overriding factor in my life.

. . . . .

Louis Nizer

Attorney; author, *My Life in Court* (Doubleday, 1961)

I find it necessary in dealing with clients, who are often under great stress, to minister to that stress before even legal advice is given.

Sometimes an epigram makes the point more effectively: "Worry is interest we pay on a debt which never comes due."

I ask my client to think of all the matters that have worried him deeply in the last year or two, and how many of those matters came to pass. Very few, if any, and when they do happen, that is time enough to worry.

I apply these precepts to myself. Trial work and legal representation are extremely stressful occupations. One cannot eliminate all the strain, but certainly by rational self-analysis, one can diminish this stress substantially.

In the turbulent world in which we live, this is a necessary nostrum for good health and survival.

. . . . .

George Mandler

Professor of psychology, University of California, San Diego; author, *Mind and Body*; *Psychology of Stress* (Norton, 1984)

Stress arises out of discrepancies and interruptions in our world. Discrepancies occur essentially because the world acts and looks different from the way we expect it to be, i.e., the way we have experienced it in the past, and we are unprepared to assimilate new information because we have not anticipated it. Interruptions occur when some action (in the broadest sense of the word) we undertake does not have the desired effect, when we fail to reach our goal, when we are blocked from achieving some particular state of ourselves in the world.

Both discrepancies and interruptions have the same effect. They produce unusual amounts of physiological stress, i.e., elevated automatic nervous-system activity.

What advice follows from that? Essentially the Boy Scout motto: Be prepared! Many years ago I was at a conference where people described the preparation of astronauts, and what was emphasized was that they went through then (and presumably now) extensive experience with all kinds of possible ways in which their flights and instruments could go wrong. One consequence was that they did not experience undue stress when some misadventure did occur. In other words, the best way to be prepared for stress is to make sure that one is prepared for discrepancies and interruptions in everyday life and work situations.

. . . . .

Gordon Parks
Photographer, movie producer; author, Born Black (Harper & Row, 1971), The Learning Tree (Fawcett, 1978)

I do only what I feel like doing—at my own free time. Therefore I never admit to stress. Perhaps by doing that I conquer it. This may seem oversimplified but, for me it works.

. . . . .

Phyllis Schlafly

Activist; attorney at law; author, *Power of Positive Women*
(Jove, 1981)

I don't have any stress, and I don't see any reason to have any stress. I meet deadlines daily and weekly. I am constantly speaking and giving interviews, often before hostile audiences. I deal with so-called stressful and challenging situations, but it is the situation that is stressful—they do not produce stress in me.

Incidentally, Ronald Reagan doesn't have any stress, either. You can tell that by looking at him.

Personally, I think stress is the result of illicit sex or other forms of guilt, such as abortion, drugs, infidelity, cheating, etc. Those who know that Jesus is their Savior don't have stress.

. . . . .

Oleg Cassini

Designer

There is nothing better for releasing tension than a good game of tennis or a round of golf.

. . . . .

Alfred M. Goodloe

President, Alfred M. Goodloe Associates, Inc.; author,
Managing Yourself (Watts, 1984)

I think it's important to know one's stress points, and take steps to break up a day to avoid too many unpleasant and tension producing experiences. While I do work long hours, I always make sure my day is filled with various pleasant events—such as reading the newspaper for a considerable length of time over breakfast, taking a leisurely lunch, reading several chapters in an interesting book and watching something exciting on TV.

I believe that daily exercise is certainly one of the most effective ways to prevent stress. I play squash and tennis four times a week, and do jogging and vigorous walking on the days I'm not engaged in one of these sports.

. . . . .

Willard Scott
ᴧᴧᴧᴧᴧᴧᴧᴧᴧᴧᴧᴧᴧᴧᴧᴧᴧᴧᴧ

Weatherman extraordinaire, NBC-TV; author, *The Joy of Living* (Ballantine, 1983), *Willard Scott's Down Home Stories* (Bobbs Merrill, 1984)

Anxiety is a killer. I think anxiety kills more people than overweight. The way to avoid it as much as possible is to have people working for you in whom you have confidence. They can help you escape an awful lot of problems.

I've been lucky in that I have two people that help me. One is Nancy Fields (at NBC). She gets me my plane tickets and reminds me what appointments I have. She keeps a calendar for me. All of that. She's so incredible. I lucked out.

All of my personal business is handled by my wife—Mary. We have a business called Mariah Enterprises. I do speeches and appearances and commercials. It's a side business. It requires quite a bit of attending to. It's awfully reassuring to have somebody involved who has a vested interest in the enterprise.

It's so tough to find accountants and business people. Not that there aren't plenty of them out there that are honest and smart. It's just that they don't make a living off of you unless you're Paul Mellon. They have to have other clients. Consequently, you don't always get the service you want.

The William Morris Agency does my commercial work. My agent there and I are on the same beam. There again I'm very lucky. In this world, there are plenty of good agents but he and I have the same temperament.

If you work with the wrong kind of people, you have stress in your life. I used to have an agent with whom I didn't work very well. And the guy was excellent. He did a good job for me. But we just didn't come in on the same beam. So we parted company. I have the good sense and the forthrightness to change things when they're not working.

. . . . .

Paoli Soleri
Architect, urban planner

I am of the opinion that we make so much about stress-pressure that we generate a cry baby society. The sport gladiator or the Rock Infant idol *under pressure* gives me nausea. What of the pressure of the mother watching her baby dying of hunger? The way to handle stress is to come down from fantasy land and lock on reality and its unforgiveness. There we will find honest pressure and coherent responses.

. . . . .

Tania Grossinger
Author, *Urban Anxiety: What It Is, What to Do About It, How to Make It Work for You* (World Almanac/Pharos, 1987)

I don't think anyone should accept stress automatically, as something that comes with the territory. That's one of the mistakes we all make. It doesn't automatically happen. You can control it. It's important not to let it control you.

One of the things to do is reexamine your priorities. We're under stress because we're frustrated that we can't find the time or the energy to enjoy the things that we sense are important to us—more time for your personal life, more time for your family, for your leisure activities.

When this happens, you have to stop a moment and say,

"Now, wait a minute, how important are these other things, anyway?"

And if you feel they really are important, you have to make it a point to do something about it. This isn't as simplistic as it sounds. Many successful people have the idea that the world won't go around without them. If they get sick for a day, if they're absent for a day, if they miss a meeting, they think the whole world is going to come to an end. These people have an inflated image of themselves.

If you're confident in yourself, you'll be able to say that it's all right not to work this Saturday or this Sunday. It's all right not to try to do everything at once. The world still goes round.

. . . . .

Marvin Mitchelson

Celebrity lawyer

Do work you really enjoy. The pleasure of accomplishing things then overcomes tension and stress.

. . . . .

Rev. Jerry Falwell

President, "The Old-Time Gospel Hour" television show

Everyone is looking for some magic formula that will enable them to escape problems, pressures, tensions, disappointments, betrayals and reversals. But the quicker we learn that we will never be smart enough to get out of trouble, or rich or powerful enough to devise means to circumvent trouble, the sooner we will learn how to be successful in life because trouble will always be our companion.

. . . . .

Kevin Daley

President, Communispond, Inc.

I make certain that all important things get done. For these, I set priorities. They're attacked.

It's important that I get some exercise every day. It's not only for the physical benefits but for my mental health as well.

Squash and tennis—those things—they're like an oasis. I enter a physical world in place of a cerebral one.

I play squash at the Princeton Club, which is not far from my office, at least three times a week, sometimes five times a week, at lunch time. That means I have to leave at 12:20, or I can't do it.

Because this is so important to me, it takes precedence over the problems and emergencies and everything else. I have to start planning to do it when I arrive in the morning. Say there's a meeting at eleven o'clock. When the meeting begins, I ask how long it's going to take. If someone says that it's going through lunch, then I say I can't make that. "I have to be out of here at 12:15," I say. The guidelines have been set up. I have prepared my exit, so to speak. (One result is that the meeting tends to run better; it doesn't dribble.)

In the summer, I play tennis every night. I leave work early, at five o'clock. I get the 5:10 train. I play tennis from 6 o'clock until quarter of eight. That's important to me. I make sure that gets done.

. . . . .

Jesse Helms

U.S. Senator (North Carolina)

I've never been plagued with stress. Oh, there are moments when I have to slip off by myself and assess criticism or defeat or other difficulty. But I've not consciously felt stress since I've been in the Senate.

I always try to remember two things:

Being a Christian, I remind myself that I am totally incapable of handling any difficult situation alone. When something difficult arises, I retreat for a few minutes to a little office I have in the Capitol, just off the rotunda. And there I pray—not that I will win, but that I may be led to do what I honestly believe is right. It works wonders for me.

I recall an episode that occurred when I was a young boy. I was in a contest at school, and it was obvious that I wasn't going to win the contest. It must have shown, because my father mentioned to me one day the he hadn't seen me smile for several days—and that I was always his "smiling boy."

I told him the situation—that I was in a contest and wasn't going to win, etc. He looked at me for a moment or so, then said: "Well, son, have you done the best you could?" I replied that I had—but that I still wasn't going to win.

Whereupon he gave me some advice that I have often quoted, and which my staff had engraved on a brass plaque which hangs on my office wall. That plaque was the nicest birthday gift I've received—the words of my father who said that day long ago:

"Son, the Lord doesn't require you to win; He just expects you to try."

That's the best antidote for stress that I can imagine.

. . . . .

Sherwin A. Kaufman, MD

Author, *Sexual Sabotage; How to Enjoy Sex in Spite of Physical & Emotional Problems* (Macmillan, 1981)

The way I have always dealt with stress is through music. (I am a pianist by avocation, a specialist in infertility by profession.)

Music can be so profound that I can only equate it with a religious experience. I have repeatedly been moved to tears by Bach, Mozart or Beethoven.

It relieves tension to know that there is an abundance of supernatural musical strains (like the poet Lermontov's "Angel"). Best of all, I am able to "tune in" at will, even if there is no audible sound. Given ear phones or a piano, I do even better.

6

Working with Other People; Delegating

There is plenty of time to get everything done—if you delegate. When you give over some of your duties to someone else, you are adding their energies to your own. A big boost in your efficiency is the immediate result. At the same time, you're able to begin concentrating on what's important. Robert H. Breckinridge, president and chief executive officer of Vitronics Corporation, one of America's fastest-growing compa-

nies, recalls once taking over a new job and being told by his boss "to make sure you are the least busy of all the people associated with you." Says Breckinridge: "By this he meant that I should organize myself and the people who worked for me so that I had the least to do on a day-to-day basis, and could spend time thinking about the actual future of the business."

FAILING TO DELEGATE

The process of delegating involves identifying the tasks that can be passed on to subordinates, finding the right person to do each task, making clear what needs to be done and then monitoring each individual's progress. While it is universally accepted that delegating is the perfect way to get more accomplished in less time, many people fail to use the art to their advantage. They wreck their efficiency and effectiveness by spending their time on jobs that could easily be done by others. "The hardest thing for people to do who rise through the management ranks is to delegate properly," says Robert H. Breckinridge. "This innate insecurity is a major cause for the poor use of time.

"In a nutshell, use your expertise when needed to get into the details, but use the expertise of others in those areas you are not necessarily competent to handle."

There are several reasons people don't delegate. Some don't even consider doing it. They're deeply involved in tasks that they have long since mastered, and they have come to feel a certain preeminence in their ability to do them. If, for example, you're the company's director of public relations, you probably have the skills to develop a needed press kit faster and better than any of your subordinates. But that doesn't mean that you should spend time writing news releases and having photos duplicated. Your subordinates can undoubtedly do these jobs adequately.

People in this kind of situation often confuse activity with productivity; they feel that as long as they're busy they're dong a good job. And their busywork often does produce a feeling of accomplishment. Don't fall into the activity trap. When you have a task to complete, the first thing to ask yourself is, "Who else can do this?"

Other managers fail to delegate assignments for the simple reason that they enjoy doing them themselves. A sales manager has been attending the same trade show in Chicago each year for several years, or ever since he joined the company. He looks upon the assignment as a chance to get away, to see old friends. But it's no longer necessary for the sales manager to be there. One of his sales representatives would be able to achieve the same results. If you find yourself in this or a comparable situation, you should ask yourself whether you are indulging yourself. Couldn't your career be better served by spending the time at your desk? Take a look at your priorities.

Other excuses for not delegating include:

Not Enough Time. Some managers fail to delegate for the simple reason that they believe they don't have the time to do it. A project has to be done right away. Delegating it would mean that the manager has to sit down with the subordinate, explain the project, establish what the goals are, get input from the subordinate as to how the goals are to be achieved, and establish controls and a deadline. There's not sufficient time for all of that, the manager feels. He ends up doing the job himself or herself.

The solution is to be sure to allot time in your daily schedule to meet with subordinates. In other words, you have to set aside delegating time. Delegating, in fact, should be at or near the top of your list when it comes to setting daily priorities.

This should be your attitude even when minor tasks are involved. Some managers feel it complicates a simple job to try to delegate it. In some cases, this may be true. But look at minor jobs as a way of developing your skill as a delegator. They'll prepare you for delegating the more grandiose projects.

Understaffing. Having an insufficient staff of overworked subordinates can be a big stumbling block when seeking to delegate. But it's not an impossible situation. Do whatever you must do in an effort to hire additional people. This can mean taking on an additional staff member or two or hiring specialists from the outside. If you're not able to add people, check the subordinates you do have. Are they using their time efficiently? Are *they* delegating to *their* subordinates? In most cases you shouldn't worry about the situation; delegate anyway. You're almost sure to find that your subordinates are flexible enough to handle the additional work.

Incompetence. Your subordinates really may not be prepared to do the tasks that you want to assign to them. They may lack both the skills and experience. Perhaps the best thing to do is make changes; replace those who are unskilled.

Another way to solve the problem is to use delegation as a form of training. Begin with the assignment of simple, routine tasks. Step by step, develop each subordinate's level of skill and competence. It takes great patience but it can be done.

Fear. Some managers, even while complaining about being overworked, will not delegate enough to ease their burdens. Their insecurity holds them back. They worry that the subordinate will do a better job than they could ever do, and win the boss's favor.

If you've ever been guilty of these feelings, you're displaying too much self-interest. You have to begin to think more of your company or your department as a team. Everyone is organized toward attaining certain goals. Everyone profits when those goals are realized.

Lack of Company Organization. Let's say your boss assigns a task to one of your subordinates without telling you. Chaos is the immediate result. You can no longer effectively delegate to that subordinate.

What you must do is sit down with your boss and come to some mutual understanding of your duties and those of each of your subordinates. Discuss the company's or department's organizational chart with him or her. Explain the confusion that results when he or she shoots from the hip in handing out assignments.

Lack of Experience. Delegating is no easy task. It involves communicating and motivating. You can improve as a delegator by doing it, by actually delegating. Don't hold back because you lack experience. The reward—doubling or tripling your output—is too great.

TASKS TO DELEGATE

Routine tasks can usually be easily passed to a subordinate. Let's say that each month you have to prepare a report that classifies customer complaints. The complaints come directly to you, and you spend a day or so each month tabulating them. This is a task that could undoubtedly be handled by a subordinate. Instruct the subordinate how to do the job. Arrange for the complaints to go directly to the subordinate. Set appropriate deadlines.

Research, scheduling and report-writing are other tasks that can usually be easily delegated. While they may seem tedious to you, they are likely to represent increased responsibility and even a step up the ladder for a subordinate.

Specialty tasks are also good to delegate. These are jobs that require the services of a skilled professional. It can be an accountant or a lawyer, a computer programmer or market researcher.

When you plan to hire an outside specialist, be sure to check the expert's qualifications, carefully. If you hire a lawyer, don't take it for granted that he or she knows real estate law. Investigate. Not every accountant is an expert on tax matters. Examine the individual's skills and experience carefully.

Once the expert starts work, be sure to maintain supervision. You should have or seek to acquire sufficient knowledge in the expert's specialized field so that you can properly monitor the work being done. Does the expert have an intelligent grasp of the problem? Have the proper goals been set? Are they being achieved? No matter the field or specialty involved, you're the one responsible until the project reaches completion.

WHAT NOT TO DELEGATE

Subordinates can be given the authority to make decisions only within certain bounds. You can't allow them to make policy decisions. That responsibility remains with you.

Certain other areas of responsibility can't be delegated, either.

For example, when a crisis develops you may be able to have your subordinates handle certain aspects of it, but the overall responsibility for any emergency remains yours.

Problems involving discipline can't be delegated, either. It's unjust and unreasonable to expect someone else to reprimand or punish in your place.

You can never delegate the bestowal of praise. You can't say to a subordinate, "Tell Howard I think he is doing a terrific job on this project, and we're very grateful for all that he's done." Howard is not likely to be very impressed. Secondhand praise, in fact, can have an effect opposite to what was intended. The individual who was to be the object of the commendation may feel hurt that his or her boss couldn't take the time to deliver the kind words in person.

HOW TO DELEGATE

When you have a task for someone else to handle, make an appointment with that person to discuss the assignment. In the meeting, tell the subordinate exactly what you expect him or her to achieve.

Be certain that the two of you agree on specific goals. Make these very clear. Encourage the subordinate to develop his or her own method for achieving the goals. Never allow the subordinate to lose sight of them.

Explain what materials and budget you're giving the person.

Be sure to establish some kind of reporting process so that you can keep abreast of the subordinate's progress. This is wise from the standpoint of organization, and also makes the subordinate aware that he or she has your support; you are there as a backup. Put a memo in your tickler file (page 121) concerning each task you give to the person.

Whenever you assign work, it's vital to give the person the power to act, to exercise initiative. You shouldn't have to tell the subordinate what to do at every stage of the project. If the subordinate keeps coming to you to ask you what to do, you may as well have done the job yourself. You want the subordinate to do the work and then report to you routinely. You can help the process by offering encouragement.

You and the subordinate should also reach an agreement as to when the task should be completed. Don't be vague about this. Don't say that the project should be finished "'sometime next month" or "when you can get to it." Establish a specific date for the project's completion.

The first time you delegate a task to an individual, give that person as much supervision as you feel is required. If the person is quick and efficient in completing the task, reduce the amount of supervision the next time you delegate the job. Begin to increase the number of duties and responsibilities you assign to the person. For instance, if you find your new secretary is a whiz at typing correspondence, begin encouraging him or her to compose letters as well. As this implies, by delegating you can upgrade the skills and experience of the people who work for you.

With big projects, you may want to use a team approach, selecting several subordinates to work together as a group. Then appoint a leader. Hold the leader responsible for the successful completion of the project. It's up to the leader to work with each of the team members, setting goals for each, getting their input, establishing controls and deadlines. The leader, obviously, has to be a skilled delegator, too.

How can you tell whether you're good at delegating? One way is by simply appraising what the next move is on any given assignment. If the next move is the subordinate's, the chances are you're doing things right. If the next move is yours, it's likely something has gone awry. If this keeps happening, you are likely to find that your subordinates are running out of work, while you're running out of time.

KEEPING DELEGATED JOBS DELEGATED

Once you've assigned a task to a subordinate, don't allow yourself to be manipulated into relieving the subordinate of the responsibility for taking the next step. This can happen in the blink of an eye. Let's say you allow yourself to be buttonholed in a hallway or the elevator. The conversation begins, "Boss, we've got a problem." The "we" implies that the subordinate believes that you and he or she are *sharing* responsibility for the next step. Say the wrong thing—such as, "Let me get back to you"—and the problem is right back on your shoulders.

How should you handle this kind of situation? By seeing to it that the next move is the subordinate's. For example, you could say to the subordinate, "You're right. There is a problem there. Give me a call tomorrow and tell me how it should be handled. What are the alternatives?" Avoid using the word "we" in your response.

Each time you hand out an assigned task, your subordinate can act in one of five different ways:

1. Do nothing until told.

2. Ask what to do.

3. Recommend action, then take it.

4. Act, then advise you immediately.

5. Act, then report to you in a routine manner.

If you're an astute delegator, you will not permit numbers one and two to occur. Do so and you'll become so occupied with what your subordinate is doing, your time will become subordinate-imposed time. You won't be able to focus on what's important to you. You're no longer in control.

Always remember that time spent in doing things *for* your subordinate is always subordinate-imposed time, says William

Oncken, Jr., author of *Managing Management Time*. Time spent doing things *with* them is always discretionary time. "Whenever possible," says Oncken, "do things with them rather than for them."

PERSONAL SERVICE COMPANIES

You, as a homeowner, aren't likely to hesitate about employing a carpenter, plumber or electrician to do a job that's necessary. The professional has the skills and equipment the job requires. When you want the lawn mowed or snow shoveled from the front walk, you probably hire a neighborhood kid.

These are tried and proven methods of saving time by offering money in its place. It's now possible to hire individuals to perform a much wider range of tiresome and time-consuming tasks.

For example, there's Services Unlimited, a company founded in 1977 by David Alwadish of New York City, that hires out people, often for a flat fee of $7.50, to take your place standing in line for such purposes as applying for a passport or paying a parking fine. In Denver, Arlys Krim, the founder of All Tasks Considered, will sit with your cats, water plants, plan your parties, pick up your dry cleaning or wait for the plumber. Road Runner in Kansas City will shop for the dress shirt you need tonight or take your car in for its annual inspection. Barbara Peters of Resources, another New York City firm, will pay your bills, organize your closets and answer your mail while you are on vacation.

Such personal service organizations advertise in local newspapers and magazines and distribute handbills proclaiming their usefulness. But most people learn of them by word of mouth.

When should you consider using such a service? Usually the best thing to do is decide how much your own time is worth. Let's say you earn $25 an hour. This means that if you spend two hours preparing food for a dinner party, the meal is costing you $50 in labor. (This assumes, of course, that you could be earning money at the time you were laboring in the kitchen.)

There's another factor to consider. Maybe you like to cook, it's relaxing for you. If that's the case, it wouldn't make sense to hire a chef. Personal service organizations are more for the tasks you loathe.

. . . . .

Additional Reading

Don't Do. Delegate!, by James M. Jenks and John M. Kelly (Watts, 1985). How-to-do-it guidance concerning the "secret power" of successful managers.

How to Get People to Do Things, by Robert Conklin (Ballantine, 1982). Strategies for application in the business world and one's personal life as well.

Winning Strategies for Managing People, by Robert Irwin and Rita Wolenik (Watts, 1985). Tips on stroking and reprimanding, promoting and demoting, hiring and firing.

Managing Management Time, by William Oncken, Jr. (Prentice-Hall, 1984). Pragmatic tips for increasing discretionary time.

7

Fighting
Procrastination

∿∿∿

"Tomorrow," says the procrastinator, "I'll get everything done. I'll come in early and write that report that was due yesterday. I'll return the phone calls from last week and start in on the mail that's piled up."

But tomorrow is no different. All the promises are simply made again.

Procrastination is rampant in the business world.

It affects both sexes and people of all ages. It devastates personal relationships, causes emotional anguish, wrecks any attempt at effectiveness and has probably ruined more careers than hard drinking.

Procrastination can color every aspect of your life. At home, it can be evidenced by letting the lawn go untrimmed or by delaying in paying household bills. At school, the procrastinator may put off doing homework or studying for tests. Students sometimes put off talking with teachers or counselors, or completing degree requirements. Your personal life may be touched by procrastinating if you find yourself putting off getting a haircut, making an appointment with the dentist or taking a vacation that you deserve. The failure to be on time for social events or to call, write or visit friends or relatives are other signs of the condition.

In the business world, procrastinators are people who are tardy for work or for meetings, the ones who put off making telephone calls for as long as possible or postpone the writing of reports or answering correspondence. The result is that their lives become filled with anxiety as they go careening from one crisis to another.

Procrastinators are neglectful about confronting problems that need solving. They delay in initiating new programs that would bring them and their departments increased recognition. And in those infrequent instances where they are entitled to recognition, they even put off asking their bosses about promotions or raises. They seem to be constantly undermining their advancement and ultimate success.

There is another and much higher price to be paid for constantly putting things off. Many procrastinators get bogged down in mediocre careers because they never get around to pursuing their goals, much less achieving them. Procrastination wipes out fulfillment. The procrastinator's fondest dreams are always on hold.

PROCRASTINATION AND STRESS

Those who are known to be procrastinators are often looked upon as being easygoing and relaxed. They don't seem to have a care. Otherwise, how could they be so indifferent about their behavior?

No such conclusion could be further from the truth. Individuals who procrastinate are, in fact, victims of stress on several different levels.

When you initially put something off, it may not bother you. But keep putting it off, and your begin to feel bad about it. You'll probably start getting mad at yourself about the delay. And the longer you keep putting it off, the more anxious and angry you become.

Procrastinators also produce stress for themselves by their panicky, last-ditch efforts to get things done. Some people work well under pressure; others don't. But everyone experiences anxiety when seeking to achieve maximum output within a limited time frame.

In addition, procrastinators trigger a great deal of stress in their relationships with other people. If you're late for a meeting or an appointment, you create tension with those affected. Anytime you fail to do something you promised to do, you risk souring a relationship. A manager who writes a sloppy report because he or she put it off until the last possible minute can make a whole department look bad. That kind of situation creates wall-to-wall bad will.

PROCRASTINATION AND SELF-DECEPTION

Very few people are willing to admit they are dyed-in-the-wool procrastinators. They won't admit it to themselves or to others.

Procrastinators become experts in self-delusion. For example, the procrastinator takes an extra half hour for lunch so he or she can "relax" before sitting down to write a report.

"I'll watch television tonight," says the procrastinator in a classic case of self-delusion, "and still have time to get my report ready for that meeting tomorrow." Another line goes, "I can stay in bed another half hour and still be at work on time."

Many procrastinators tell themselves that they will complete a particular job when they're "in the mood." What they fail to understand is that their moods are produced by their actions. Waiting for inspiration to strike is inevitably a wait with no end.

If you're sometimes guilty of such self-delusion, resolve to keep a record, an absolutely honest record, of what you actually do for an entire week. Don't leave out a single thing. Include the time you spend sleeping and commuting, the hours you devote to meals; your work hours, with a breakdown of time spent at meetings, on the telephone and doing paperwork. Put down how you spend your leisure time, whether it goes toward napping or watching TV, jogging or attending movies. How much time do you spend reading the daily newspaper or magazines? (Also see the time audit in Chapter 2, pp. 50–53.)

At the end of the week, you may be surprised at the amount of time you spend putting things off. Maybe the diary will reveal that you've become a paper shuffler, moving pieces of correspondence and memos from one stack to another without really ever acting on anything. Maybe you'll come to realize that you're spending several hours in front of the television set each week, staring at it just because it happens to be on. Such a diary is an important first step.

THE ROOTS OF PROCRASTINATION

Overcoming procrastination is no easy matter. In an effort to make a real dent in the habit, first try to come to some understanding of its psychological roots.

"Most procrastinators think they are lazy, disorganized or don't care about their work, but that's a myth," says Dr. Jane B. Burka, a psychologist at the University of California/Berkeley and a co-author (with Dr. Leonara M. Yuen) of *Procrastination; Why You Do It, What to Do About It.* "In fact, procrastinators are often so concerned with their work that they're afraid to get started. Procrastination is their way of dealing with pressure."

Dr. Burka and other specialists have spotlighted several causes for procrastination. They include:

Fear of Failure. Procrastinators dream impossible dreams. They set unrealistic goals for themselves and they feel overwhelmed that they are unable to achieve them. Discouraged, they either put off doing a task, and keep putting it off, or they do it with a last-ditch burst of frantic effort. They never really put their skills to the test, which is their underlying aim.

Fear of Success. A person who is competent and effective courts success and the changes that accompany it. Some people are apprehensive about these changes, which can include increased recognition, a promotion, or more authority and more responsibility. These people are comfortable; they prefer the status quo. The result is that they subvert their success through procrastination. They retreat from competition.

Rebellion. A teenager leaves his or her room messy. A student is late for class. A housewife puts off calling a repairman to fix a leaky faucet. An accountant at a large company delays billing suppliers. These people are using procrastination as an act of insubordination. They're sending a message to whatever authority figure looms large in their lives. They're attracting attention to themselves. They're saying, "I'm important; I count."

Lack of Problem-solving Skills. Some people simply haven't developed the ability to cope with the challenges the workplace presents. They lack training and experience in organizing their work and monitoring their time. They can't get started on any really important task because they're so occupied with trivial matters. These are often people who say "yes" to every demand made upon their time.

You have to make up your mind about what tasks are important to you, and then decide how each one is to be accomplished. You have to learn to say "no" to individuals who come to you with requests that are going to rob you of your time. (Also see "Saying No" in Chapter 3, p. 81–82.)

Perfectionism. "The urge to do everything perfectly is the essence of the good little girl," *Working Woman* magazine noted recently. "Perfectionism," the magazine said, "is a quality that women have in abundance."

The perfectionist measures performance against some dimly defined standard that's almost impossible to achieve. Doing something merely adequately is not sufficient. There's no middle ground. The perfectionist must either do the job flawlessly or not do it at all.

Because the perfectionist has such a deep-seated fear of not being able to do anything right, he or she never gets anything done. When a report has to be written, the perfectionist doesn't get beyond the first paragraph because he or she can't stop crossing out sentences that fail to reach his or her lofty standards. The report keeps getting postponed as a result. It's finally written just before the deadline but too hurriedly to reflect the caliber of work that he or she is really capable of.

OVERCOMING PROCRASTINATION

Learning to overcome self-doubt is the most effective thing you can do in attempting to stamp out the procrastination in your life. You're not going to change overnight, of course. But try to become more confident and more decisive. Try thinking of yourself as a doer.

It also helps to have a number of different techniques at your fingertips and choose the one that applies to your situation. It really isn't important which method you use as long as it's *some* method. "Most people have no plan at all for coping with the temptation to procrastinate," says Edwin C. Bliss, author of *Doing It Now,* "except for the sheer use of will power—which usually doesn't work."

Here are some tried and proven methods for tackling the procrastination problem:

Attack in Stages. Let's say you've identified a big chunk of wasted time in your daily schedule. Don't attempt to do anything drastic about it. You're not going to give up the habit of watching late-night movies on television or talking with your friends on the telephone simply by making a promise to do so. Instead, attack on a piecemeal basis. You're much more likely to be successful.

Let's say that you watch junk programming on television four or five nights a week from around 6:30 to 8:00. Divide the time period in half. The first half should be devoted toward achieving a specific goal—writing the draft of a memo or report, or teaching yourself speed reading; straightening out a drawer or a closet or just washing the evening dishes. The second half of the time period is yours to waste. Revert to form if you wish, watching local news on TV or reruns of "Mary Tyler Moore." That's your reward. Gradually, you may be able to carve out more and more useful time.

Prepare Daily "To Do" Lists. Each morning jot down several things you want to accomplish that day. Establish priorities and cross off each item as you complete it. You'll get a sense of achievement from this. "I have found that one difference between people at the top of the ladder and people at the bottom is that those at the top use a To Do list every day to make better use of their time; those at the bottom don't," says Alan Lakein in *How to Get Control of Your Time and Your Life.*

Delegate. If you can give some of your duties to someone else, then it will lighten your load and give you more time to concentrate on the important tasks. But most procrastinators find it difficult to delegate. "I'm the only one who can do the job," is the excuse they use. Granted, the person you assign to do a job won't do it exactly the way you might have, but realize that there may be an advantage in having the job done a different way. (For more on delegating, see Chapter 6.)

Divide Big Jobs into Little Ones. This tried and proven technique is alien to most procrastinators, whose goal it is to complete only tasks of earth-shaking proportions. But it's highly effective. The idea is to break any large job into bits and pieces, then tackle only a small part of the project each day. Start with a task that is going to give you a feeling of accomplishment, and go on from there, completing one step at a time until the job is finished. The daily efforts add up fast.

This approach can be applied to almost any job that needs doing. "Let's say you're a procrastinator and you want to clean out your files," says Terry Davidson, a cofounder of Procrastinators Anonymous. "You can't say, 'OK, this goes out! That goes out!' That's too much to ask of a procrastinator.

"Instead, make several different categories for what's in the files. In one pile, put everything you intend to refile; in another, what you may want to refile; in a third, what you may want to discard, and in the fourth, what you definitely want to throw out. Everything in the fourth category should be placed in a paper bag or cardboard box. The accumulation of items will give you a feeling of satisfaction. I use a shopping bag for what I'm going to throw away. As it begins filling up, I feel wonderful. If I had just tossed the things in a wastebasket, I wouldn't have this little triumph. Sometimes I get out the bathroom scale and weigh the bag. I'm able to say, 'Wow! I'm throwing out ten pounds of stuff!' It makes me feel like throwing out even more."

Use Self-exhortation. Edwin C. Bliss, author of *Doing It Now,* advises overcoming procrastination with a technique called "Tape Talk." It involves simply talking like a "dutch uncle" into a cassette recorder, urging yourself to do this or that task. "Just verbalizing your feelings often breaks the logjam," Bliss says. "You can save the tape and play it back from time to time when you need a 'talking to' by the world's foremost authority on you: yourself.

"It sounds off-the-wall," Bliss says, "but it works."

Don't Waste Time Feeling Guilty. Guilt feelings are pandemic among procrastinators. Anytime you start doubting yourself, do something—and do it right away!

One of the most important things you can do in your struggle to tame procrastination is to resolve to make every day count. Before you arise in the morning, ask yourself, "What is one goal I want to achieve this day?" Make up your mind to use your time and energy to attain that goal. No matter what, don't put it off.

. . . . .

Additional Reading

Procrastination; Why You Do It, What to Do About It, by Jane B. Burka, PhD, and Leonara M. Yuen, PhD (Addison-Wesley, 1983). A comprehensive handbook explaining time-tested techniques on how to *manage* procrastination.

8

Making Leisure Count

People who work smart should also play smart. It's great to be competitive and goal-oriented on the job, to be constantly striving to beat the clock, but when it comes to your leisure you need to lighten up. Most people don't. Their leisure is a form of labor. Take the fitness craze. The muscle builders groan from pumping iron. "No pain, no gain," they say. "Go for the burn," urges Jane Fonda in her fitness tapes.

Joggers chart their daily progress in the same manner they keep track of profits and sales at the office.

Such attitudes hardly encourage the idea of "losing a sense of oneself" that many sociologists consider the basis of leisure. But the truth is that many Americans simply don't know how to relax and get away from it all. "To do nothing is suspect in our culture," says Dr. Geoffrey L. Godbey, professor of recreation and parks at Pennsylvania State University. "There are still some people who know how to do nothing but we define them as failures."

Dr. Godbey offers these suggestions to those who take a too-serious approach to life:

• Hang around with kids and dogs; they're often playing.
• Practice laughing at yourself. Make fun of your foibles.
• When you exercise, do something that's fun—play basketball or go roller skating.
• Do things you love to do even if they appear absurd to others.

Part of the problem is that some people hate to admit that they're capable of having any leisure time. It's almost as if the concept of leisure carried a stigma. "The ghost of the work ethic is always with us," says H. Douglas Sessom, author of *Leisure Services* and a professor of recreation administration at the University of North Carolina. "People have to have tangible benefits—how many miles run, pounds lost, a tan."

The word "idle" is often applied in a derogatory sense; "lazy" and "slothful" are two of its synonyms. Women, especially, tend to define the word that way. K.C. Cole, in her book, *Between the Lines: Searching for the Space between Feminism and Femininity and Other Tight Spots,* says that women "seem to have a hard time accepting the legitimacy of time spent doing anything that doesn't directly relate to a payback or a clean child or a cooked meal." She quotes a successful financial executive who, in her 40s, finally realized that regular exercise and massage were not frills. The woman said: "It's often part of a male executive's life to play squash or tennis and then get a massage, which they call a rubdown. I realized I needed this, too, to survive. But you'd be surprised how many women in my position say they'd like to do that, but they can't find the time."

The leisure problem has been exacerbated by our modern society in which, for many, work and leisure overlap. According to the *Wall Street Journal,* this trend stems from the ever-increasing emphasis on a service economy. The newspaper profiled an unemployed Pittsburgh steelworker who eventually started his own home improvement business. At the steel mill, he normally put in "a straight 40-hour week," forgetting about his job as soon as his shift ended. But in his new role he worked nearly 100 hours a week, often meeting prospective customers in the evening or on weekends, periods that he had previously devoted to softball, fishing or other leisure time activities. He told the *Journal* that he enjoyed being his own boss and the fact that he wasn't always being told what to do. But one virtue of blue-collar life, he recalled, was the sharp distinction between free time and work.

Still another reason that leisure is difficult to achieve is that there just aren't as many leisure hours as there used to be. A 1986 *Wall Street Journal*-NBC News Survey revealed that twice as many Americans claim to have less leisure than they used to than those who claim to have more.

The newspaper quoted statistics showing that the 40-hour work week, protected by federal law for nearly 50 years, is a myth for many wage earners. During 1985, professionals and managers worked an average of 45 hours a week. Manufacturing employees totaled an average of 43 hours.

U.S. corporations are helping to contribute to the squeeze on leisure. Although many companies continue to offer subsidies for health-club memberships and adult education courses, such benefits began to be trimmed during the mid-1980s, falling victim to the competitive economy. The *Wall Street Journal,* quoting Fred Best, a California business consultant who had studied corporate leisure, reported that "human resources just aren't high on the agenda."

Finally, technology is transforming the way leisure activities are pursued, and the changes aren't always beneficial. VCR presentations are now the frequent background to living room conversation and the evening meal. Tape cassettes are changing reading from a thoroughly relaxing pastime to one that you can pursue while driving to work in the morning.

For many people, the first real chance to relax comes with retirement. Richard Bolles, author of *What Color Is Your Parachute,* a best-selling book about job hunting and career choices, says that we have come to think of leisure as "a postponed activity." Although only one out of four Americans work until the mandatory retirement age of 70, "the big joke in our culture is the heart attack that comes a week before the big cruise you've worked for all your life," Bolles says. His latest book, *The Three Boxes of Life,* cries out against the division of life into, first, education; then, work; and finally, retirement.

For many, it's important that their leisure involve a change of pace, that it be relaxing. Or perhaps you want to use it to make a positive contribution to your life or to the lives of others. The point is that meaningful leisure experiences don't just happen. You have to follow a blueprint.

PLANNING YOUR LEISURE

Most people follow one of two patterns in their use of leisure time. Among young professionals, the Thank-God-It's-Friday syndrome is common. After a week of stressful work, they relax like mad on weekends. They might party with friends or plan a special getaway. These are the people who take raft trips or try hang-gliding or hot-air ballooning.

What they're doing is overcompensating for the stress they encounter at work. Escape is the sole purpose of their weekend.

The other leisure pattern followed by people in high-stress jobs involves minimal activity and passive entertainment. They sleep late on Saturdays and Sundays, then often lounge around, listening to music or in front of the television set. They might sunbathe, visit on the telephone with friends, browse in a bookstore or go to the movies.

Both the thrill seekers and the weekend sluggards return to

work rested and revivified on Monday morning. They accomplished what they set out to accomplish. But neither group has considered the many other leisure options they have. They don't realize that there are possibilities for personal or career development that can provide them with just as much relief and relaxation as partying until dawn or two hours before their VCR. They're stuck in a leisure rut. Often all it takes to get out of the rut is an awareness of alternative leisure time activities—be they sports, continuing education, community service, or cultural activities.

In choosing a leisure-time activity that is suited to your temperament, begin by pinpointing your preferences in general terms. Do you prefer indulging in solitary pursuits or would you rather be one of a group? If it's the latter, do you prefer the group be made up of friends or family members?

Do you want to be stimulated or do you want to relax? Some people seek the risks involved in such activities as hang-gliding or mountaineering. Others prefer that their excitement come in the form of murder mysteries or crossword puzzles.

Should the activity provide you with physical benefits or would you rather pick something passive? What sports do you enjoy? Are you interested in the competition offered by tennis, squash, golf? Or do you prefer those sports that are sometimes labeled "cooperative," such as canoeing, horseback riding, skiing, hiking, and swimming and going to the beach? Then there are the spectator sports, baseball, football and auto racing among them.

Some people actually suffer through their vacation experiences. Their high expectations never come close to being fulfilled and they return home fatigued and frustrated. This can happen when you pick a vacation spot or activity because a friend recommends it or on the basis of a travel agent's flashy brochure. Try instead to be guided by your personality and interests.

YOUR JOB AND YOUR LEISURE

You should also choose your leisure activities on the basis of your job and what it offers—or fails to offer. Let's say you're under tremendous pressure during your working hours. You whiz through each day in kind of a blur. You might then consider spending your vacation reading or model-building or, if you enjoy vacation travel, in quiet sightseeing.

If boredom is a problem where you work, you'll probably want to seek out stimulation when you plan your leisure. How about surfing or a raft trip, scuba diving or sport parachuting? A computer programmer from New York City took a two-week vacation in Lime Rock, Connecticut, so he could attend the Skip Barber's Racing Drivers School at the track there.

If your job involves a great deal of travel, maybe it would be a good idea to stay around home during your vacation. But do something different. Buy a home computer and start charting stock market trends. If your job fails to provide you with any intellectual enrichment, maybe you can get it from your leisure time.

You can also use your leisure to help you in achieving whatever goals you have set for yourself. In terms of your career, you can use your free time to increase your knowledge of your field or a related field, perhaps enrolling in an adult education course (see below) or setting up a reading program for yourself.

When it comes to your financial goals, you can devote your leisure to pinpointing real estate or other investment opportunities. A book editor I know deals in antiques in his spare time.

Your leisure offers enormous potential, both personally and professionally. It's up to you to recognize and pursue the opportunities available.

SHAPING UP

If your leisure hours don't include a plan for regular exercise, you should consider adopting one. A study conducted at Purdue University in 1984 tested a group of originally sedentary men and women before and after a nine-month program of regular exercise. After that period, the group was found to be 70% better at making complex decisions, a skill measured by a standardized test using flash cards. (A control group of people who already exercised regularly retained the same skills throughout the nine months and with no change.)

There can be no doubt about it—muscular strength and cardio-respiratory stamina will better enable you to cope with the problems and the stress of work. Being fit is working smart; it gives you a psychological edge.

Begin by assessing the shape you are now in. If you're not sure, consult a book such as *The U.S. Army Fitness Program*. It offers the Army Physical Readiness Test, which all soldiers, male and female, must take twice a year. The test consists of a two-mile run, two minutes of push-ups and two minutes of sit-ups. A table in the book rates results from "superior" to "very poor," with separate ratings for men and women. For instance, superior men between the ages of 22 and 26 are expected to do between 56 and 65 push-ups and run two miles in 12 to 13 minutes. Superior women are expected to do 31 to 40 push-ups and take 15-16 minutes for the run.

As you get older, the standards are not as strict. Men 42 to 46 years old are rated superior if they can do 40 to 47 push-ups in two minutes and run two miles in 14 minutes and 12 seconds to 15 minutes. Superior women in the 42 to 46 age group have to be able to do 22 to 29 push-ups; they have three more minutes to complete the run.

Fitness testing is also one of the features of the aerobics exercise programs developed by Dr. Kenneth Cooper. In fact, it was Dr. Cooper who, perhaps more than anyone else, brought aerobics to international attention. In his book, *Aerobics,* first published in 1968, Cooper established basic principles and set guidelines for public participation in aerobics, a term he applied to a variety of exercises that stimulate the heart and lungs for a period of time "sufficiently long to produce beneficial changes in the body." Running, swimming, cycling and jogging are the exercises Cooper recommends. His exercise programs are the official programs of the U.S. Air Force, U.S. Navy and Royal Canadian Air Force.

"Men and women up to 30 years of age can pursue any type of exercise they want," Cooper says. "Just choose one you enjoy." He says you can start exercising if you've had a medical checkup within the past year, and the doctor found nothing wrong with you.

Between the ages of 30 and 50, you still have a choice of sports, says Cooper, but if you plan to do strenuous exercises be sure to get your doctor's specific approval.

Cooper's books (described at the end of this chapter) offer detailed instructions on how to participate in an aerobics program tailored to your age and fitness category.

If such a test demonstrates that you're not in very good shape—a condition you may also discover on a frantic dash to make a train or by lugging a heavy briefcase across town when you couldn't get a taxi—you should embark on a serious exercise program, devoting about 30 minutes a day to it, three or four times a week. (If you're 35 years old or older, be sure to consult a doctor before beginning any such program.)

Tailor your program to your lifestyle and temperament. For some people, morning is the best time of day for a workout. Others may find exercising at the end of the day serves as an excellent stress reliever.

Whenever you decide to do it, treat it like an appointment or meeting; that is, write it down on your calendar.

It's also a good idea to try to enlist the aid of your spouse or a good friend. The "buddy system" helps you in keeping your commitments. For example, by making an appointment with someone to jog in the park, you are more likely to follow through on the plan than if you merely promise yourself you'll do it. Getting someone else involved is also helpful if you're planning to diet or quit smoking.

ALTERNATIVE EXERCISE PROGRAMS

Many people suffer anguish at the very thought of jogging or sitting on a stationary bike and pedaling away or swimming laps in a pool. Their personalities are not in tune with such activities; they're bored by them.

But getting in shape can involve any one of a great number of activities. Indeed, there is a wider variety to choose from than ever before. There are such standbys as tennis and horseback riding. You can join an aerobics class, a squash club or a YMCA basketball team. A recent article in *Savvy* magazine described a congressional aide in Washington, D.C., who pursued speed-canoeing as an avocation, a microbiologist in Cypress, California, who was a weekend windsurfer, and a human resources director from Minneapolis who kept in shape by rock climbing.

Take plenty of time to choose an exercise program that suits your needs and capabilities. A sport that can provide enormous benefits for one person can be an absolute disaster for another.

What is your specific objective? Do you want the program to help you relax and reduce stress? Increase your stamina? Lose weight? Build muscle strength? Become more flexible?

Experts classify exercises in five categories. In isometric exercise—typified by tightening the abdominal muscles for 20 seconds—muscles are contracted without moving the joints or extremities. Isometric exercise can build muscle size and strength, but rates poorly in terms of cardiovascular benefits.

In isotonic exercise, muscles are contracted and joints and extremities moved. Weight lifting and calisthenics are typical isotonic exercises. Like isometrics, isotonic exercises build muscle size and strength but offer only limited benefits to the cardiovascular system.

In isokinetic exercise, strength is used to lift and lower a weight. This is the principle upon which Nautilus and Universal gym equipment is based. Isokinetic exercises can benefit the cardiovascular system when they are performed in series and timed so that there are only short rest intervals between each.

Anaerobic (without oxygen) exercises—such as sprinting—are those that do not fully utilize the air that the exerciser breathes. In these spurts of activity, exhaustion usually strikes within the first couple of minutes, precluding any aerobic benefits.

Aerobic exercises are those that are fueled by oxygen and that stimulate the body system that channel it. They include rapid walking, jogging, cycling, running, swimming, cross country skiing and aerobic dancing. These are the exercises that strengthen the heart and increase the capacity of the lungs.

Aerobic exercises are also the best for burning calories and building endurance. It is believed that they lessen the chance of premature coronary heart disease or related vascular ailments.

And there are other benefits. "After a workout, the fog clears," says an office worker who jogs at lunch time. "I can go back to my desk and focus on what I'm doing."

For building strength, weight lifting or a Nautilus program are best. To increase body flexibility, you can select from among gymnastics, yoga and modern dance.

Whatever type of exercise you choose, it must be enjoyable. If it requires too much effort or tends to bore you, your chances of success are slim.

Getting your body in shape also means improving your eating habits. Try to make at least one positive change in your diet each week. Have your food grilled rather than sautéed. Skip dessert unless it's fresh fruit. Have Perrier or a wine spritzer instead of your usual luncheon drink. (For more on diet, see "Eating Right" in Chapter 5, p. 142.)

Don't try to revamp your life all at once. Set reasonable goals you can meet. Slow and steady will get you there.

GETTING SCHOOLING

If you're seeking to further your education or get training in a specific skill, you probably don't have to look beyond the company you work for. American firms are investing about $30 billion a year to educate their employees in formal classes.

Business involvement in education is not new. But between 1980 and 1985, with greater competition from abroad and changing technology at home, a much greater emphasis came to be placed on employee education as American companies sought to boost productivity. For example, by 1986, Motorola was requiring all departments to spend at least 1.5% of their payroll totals on education or return those funds to the company treasury. IBM was spending $900 million a year on education.

Business likes to do its own educating because courses can be tailored for specific job applications, whereas universities traditionally offer the theoretical basis for knowledge. Another factor is that companies like to schedule classes at their own and their employee's convenience, without being tied to the September-to-May cycle that universities follow.

If you're planning on using your leisure to get additional schooling, you'll probably be able to do it without leaving your company's offices. But even if your firm doesn't offer educational training, there are likely to be many other opportunities in your area for getting the schooling you're seeking. Begin by investigating adult-education programs. Simply call a local high school or the board of education. Also consult the Yellow Pages of your telephone directory. Look for an "Adult Education" listing under the "Schools" heading.

There are about 700 community colleges and junior colleges throughout the country, most of which allow prospective students to enroll on a part-time basis. There are evening classes. Since many of these institutions receive funds from local or state governments, tuition fees are usually much lower than those charged by four-year institutions.

The extension service is a type of adult education that many universities offer in addition to their regular programs. The courses offered (frequently meant to help professionals keep up with developments in their field) are normally intended for students who are unable to attend the university proper, often because they live too great a distance from the campus. So the school, in effect, comes to them; it "extends" itself. Colleges and universities in every state offer extension services.

VACATION TRAVEL

Travel is a leisure-time activity that can be tailored to fit almost every person's goals. You can travel alone or with others. You can use it to relax or get stimulated. It can be as structured or as nonstructured as you like. If you prefer structure in your life, you're likely to feel happy with a vacation tour in which transportation, lodging, meals and sightseeing excursions are all arranged in advance.

No matter how structured you are, don't make the common mistake of trying to squeeze too much into one vacation—the if-it's-Tuesday-it-must-be-Belgium syndrome. If you create plans that are too elaborate, the vacation can become more stressful than the job you left behind.

When making plans, always allow for whim and spontaneity, says Stephen Birnbaum, author of a series of travel books. "The greatest pleasures of travel come from unexpected, serendipitous encounters," he says.

If you're having difficulty deciding where to spend a vacation, get the *Specialty Travel Index,* a 102-page booklet that includes everything from bicycle tours in Europe to fishing expeditions in the Colorado Rockies. Published twice a year, the index costs $5 for both issues. Write to Specialty Travel Index, 9 Mono Ave., Fairfax, CA 94930.

If you prefer to vacation within the borders of the United States, check your local bookstore or library for a copy of the *Rand McNally Destination Vacation.* Created by Hoyle Products in cooperation with the well-known mapmaker, the guidebook includes 216 vacation destinations. It costs $14.95.

· · · · ·

Additional Reading

Free Time, Making Your Leisure Count, by Jan Gault (Wiley, 1983). Practical advice on how to make leisure time more relaxing and enriching.

Leaving the Office Behind, by Barbara Mackoff (Dell, 1984). More than 100 tips for protecting your private life.

The U.S. Army Total Fitness Program, by Lt. Col. Robert E.

Hales, MD (Ballantine, 1986). The Army's fitness program tailored for the needs of busy civilians.

Aerobics, by Kenneth H. Cooper, MD (Bantam, 1980). The world's most popular fitness program.

The New Aerobics, by Kenneth H. Cooper, MD (Bantam, 1981). Exercise programs that are "age-adjusted" to the capabilities of men and women.

The Aerobic Program for Total Well-Being, by Kenneth H. Cooper, MD (Bantam, 1983). A complete program for physical, emotional and nutritional well-being.

EXPERT ADVICE

There are hundreds of different ways to relax and get away from it all. You can use your leisure to pursue flower arranging or sport parachuting, weight lifting or stamp collecting, traveling to the Orient or fixing up your house. If you're Charlotte Ford, you relax by cleaning house. Yoko Ono watches sunrise and sunset. *New York Times* publisher Arthur Ochs Sulzberger unwinds by fishing for salmon or, when he can't get to the great outdoors, he has a drink in the back room with "some of the boys." Walter Cronkite sails. Editor and author Kathy Keeton raises dogs.

However, for some of the "experts" who describe their free-time activities below, relaxing has nothing to do with getting away from it all or shifting gears from work. Isaac Asimov insists that for him "work is *not* being busy at the typewriter." And Julia Child renews herself by doing what she does best—sharing good food and wine with friends.

What relaxes Henry Kissinger (reading mystery novels) would no doubt bore astronaut James McDivitt, who prefers hiking, camping, hunting and just working in his yard. And very possibly, what relaxes you would bore both of them. Part of working smart means using your leisure in a way that best suits your personality, your income and your talents. Of course, it's always fun to open yourself to something new. In planning what to do with your precious free time, take the experts' advice as a spur to your imagination.

· · · · ·

Thomas H. Gonser
ᴠᴠᴠᴠᴠᴠᴠᴠᴠᴠᴠᴠᴠᴠᴠᴠᴠᴠᴠᴠᴠᴠᴠᴠ

Executive director and chief operating officer, American Bar Association

A significant portion of my leisure time is spent working on my personal computer, a Leading Edge. I have two areas of interest. One is in developing dispute resolution software that would assist people in reaching a fair and amicable resolution to a potential or existing dispute. The other interest is in refining software I created several years ago to analyze the economic consequences of a particular piece of litigation.

· · · · ·

Charlotte Ford
ᴠᴠᴠᴠᴠᴠᴠᴠᴠᴠᴠᴠᴠᴠᴠᴠ

Designer and socialite

Believe it or not, when I need to relax or get my thoughts together in an orderly manner, I usually set about wholehearted "house cleaning." In fact, I am a "clean freak" and enjoy very much indulging in this chore. Having expended many hours of time and energy cleaning, I find it has given me exhilaration as well as allowed me to forget problems. It's like skiing—no time to think about anything else.

Other than my bent for cleaning, I enjoy reading immensely. This again provides me with the luxury of relaxation as well as pleasure.

. . . . .

Craig Claiborne

Columnist; author, *Craig Claiborne's New York Times Cook Book* (Harper, 1961), *Cooking with Herbs & Spices* (Harper, 1984)

After a hot sauna, late each afternoon, an ice cold shower and a scotch on the rocks, I haven't a worry left.

. . . . .

James MacGregor Burns

Historian; author, *Government by the People; National, State, Local* (Basic, 1985)

My best way to relax and get away from it all is to go skiing—but also to indulge in something I call "skreading," a term I invented. Skreading is reading on ski lifts going up, and skiing down. A great combination!

. . . . .

Arthur Ochs Sulzberger

Publisher, *The New York Times*

My favorite form of relaxation is fishing—particularly salmon fishing, but any type will do in a pinch. Unfortunately, I don't get as much time as I would like to devote to this sport.

My other relaxing activity is puttering around in the garden and woods. It is an activity that really makes me forget everything that is going on in the world.

Finally, sitting in the back room with some of the boys finishing off a bottle of white wine can't be all bad.

. . . . .

Bayard Rustin
President, A. Philip Randolph Educational Fund

In my leisure time I collect antiques, mostly religious items from
Europe. I also have a collection of African art and over two
hundred walking sticks. I find that seeking out these items is very
relaxing as well as educational for me. It is also something I can do
during free time when traveling on business. When I am at my
home and wish to relax, I listen to classical music, particularly the
works of Bach.

. . . . .

John Fanning
Chairman of the board and president, Uniforce Temporary
Personnel, Inc.; author, *Work When You Want to Work* (Pocket
Books, 1985)

I'm a ferocious reader in my leisure time. I read nonfiction almost
exclusively. I think I've read everything that's ever been written
on Lincoln and the Civil War. Theology has great appeal to me,
too, Eastern as well as Western theologies.

I enjoy reading about business management. I've read every
one of Peter Drucker's books at least two or three times. I also read
about fifteen magazines a month.

I've been an owner of harness racing horses for twenty-five or
so years. My stable is housed at one of three tracks, Roosevelt
Raceway, Yonkers Raceway or Monticello. Harness racing is a
different universe for me. When I'm at the races, I don't think
about Uniforce, my wife or kids or anything.

Third, there's my family. We go to the theatre whenever it's
possible. That's very relaxing to me.

Vacations have never been important to me. A weekend can be

a tremendous rejuvenator. When I arrive at the office on Monday morning, I'm ready to knock down stone walls!

. . . . .

Denton A. Cooley, MD

Surgeon, Texas Heart Institute

I have always advocated the well-rounded life, including necessary attention to work, rest and recreation. For recreation I engage in a number of activities. I have a ranch close to Houston and enjoy going there for a variety of activities including horseback riding, tennis and walking. My favorite sports are golf and tennis. Whenever I have the opportunity I engage in one or both of these sports especially on weekends. It seems to relieve my mind and stress to become involved in a highly competitive game involving physical exertion. Another enjoyable thing for me is reading. While I have little time during my work week, I travel a lot and always carry books along to read on the plane. I enjoy fiction and nonfiction, both of which seem to give me a release from daily duties.

. . . . .

Fran Manushkin

Author, *Baby, Come Out!* (Harper, 1973), *Buster Loves Buttons* (Harper, 1985), *White Rabbit's Baby Brother* (Crown, 1986)

I relax by bird-watching; I'm a birder. I live in New York City and I do my writing in a studio in Greenwich Village. Before I go there in the morning or on the way home, I usually stop in Central Park and visit The Ramble, the heavily wooded section where the birds are found.

When I look at birds on the way to work, it sets up the whole day for me; it gives me a sense of peace.

The year round birds we see are the starling, house sparrow, robin, blue jay, woodpecker and cardinal. A couple of pigeons hang out there, too. In the winter, chickadees, nuthatches and titmice come. Migrant birds visit in the spring and fall.

I'll look at the bird nests, too. I can see the mothers raising their young. In the late summer, I can see the fledglings learning to fly.

A raccoon lives there, also a woodchuck, a rabbit and bullfrogs. It's like having access to a mysterious world.

It's something you can do all year round. In the winter, I go and feed the birds. The titmice and chickadees eat out of your hand if there's snow on the ground. It's enchanting.

I learned to bird in Central Park about four or five years ago. All the experts are there, including people from the Museum of Natural History, who come and bird during lunch hour. People there tell you what you're looking at if you aren't sure. You don't need a field manual.

I never know exactly what birds I'm going to see; it's always a surprise. But even if there are only a few birds, the experience enables me to get out by myself. I'm in another world. I feel as if I'm in the country, as if I escaped from New York. That's the beauty of it.

. . . . .

Vincent Gardenia

Actor

My leisure time is spent in Italy, London, Spain and France. When I'm not working, I don't know what to do with myself.

. . . . .

Henry Morgan

Comedian

Leisure is something I am often at. One thing I do with it is compare word usages from different sources and study their interconnections. These will end up as a series of pieces for National

Public Radio, although they are not yet aware of it. Owing to the giant success of the radio series, a book will follow.

During some of my spare time, I wonder about a word processor.

Do I need one?

Will I die before anything comes of it?

Over the years I have enjoyed making train models but the suppliers, no doubt to accommodate the young, have made less and less interesting kits, the wood and metal have all turned to plastic, etc., etc. But I keep on with them anyway. Fact is, I'll make a model of almost anything.

I do double crostics. Buy them by the book. Love 'em dearly.

Used to collect oriental things but ran out of room. And the prices became absurd.

I am about to start as a volunteer at a hospital one day a week. I despise hospitals, having spent too much time in them as a patient, but I figure I owe this service. Too many volunteers I saw are creepy. I am not.

· · · · ·

Yoko Ono

Poet; singer; painter; sculptor; filmmaker; author, *John Lennon; The Summer of 1980* (Perigee, 1983)

Watching sunrise, sunset, the sky and the horizon.

· · · · ·

Willard Scott

Weatherman extraordinaire, NBC-TV; author, *The Joy of Living* (Ballantine, 1983), *Willard Scott's Down Home Stories* (Bobbs Merrill, 1984)

The only hobby I have is a garden, an orchard. It's at our home in Delaplane, Virginia, where we've lived for twenty-six years. It's huge—60 feet by 300 feet. It's got about seventy fruit trees.

I can't do much any more, but I still take care of the garden. It's a great feeling to stand there with a Jack Daniels in your hand at five-thirty or six o'clock in the afternoon, when the sun starts to move behind the Blue Ridge Mountains, and every row is neat and there's not a weed in it, and the ground is cultivated, and to know that *I* did it—me and God.

· · · · ·

Bernhardt J. Hurwood

Columnist, McNaught Syndicate; author, *My Savage Muse*; *The Story of My Life*: *Edgar Allen Poe* (Everest House, 1979), *Writing Becomes Electronic, Successful Authors Tell How They Write in the Age of the Computer* (Contemporary Books, 1986)

One of my favorite ways of goofing off—when work has really piled up—is to go to a local supermarket. I wander around, I price things, I watch the shoppers and I check out new products and the imports. Sometimes I go to more than one store and comparison shop. (There are three supermarkets within easy walking distance of where we live.) The wide range of prices is amazing. So not only am I having fun, I'm saving money! It's the art of creative procrastination. It does wonders for me. When I get back home, I'm rejuvenated, and I can plunge right in and do whatever has been waiting for me.

· · · · ·

Gene Kelly

Actor

I use an old-fashioned method to relax—reading a book.

· · · · ·

J. Bennett Johnson

U.S. Senator (Louisiana)

As an avid tennis player (and jogger whenever tennis is not possible), I have found that this kind of recreation contributes in a variety of ways—better health and physical stamina, greater self-confidence, improved concentration—to my performance on the job and in other areas of my life.

· · · · ·

Julia Child

Cooking teacher; author, *The French Chef Cookbook* (Bantam, 1979), *Julia Child & Company* (Knopf, 1978), *Julia Child & More Company* (Knopf, 1978), *From Julia Child's Kitchen* (Knopf, 1982)

Good wine, good home-cooked food with good company always renews me.

· · · · ·

John Jakes

Author, *The Seekers* (Jove, 1983), *The Lawless* (Jove, 1984), *Love & War* (Dell, 1985), *The Titans* (Jove, 1985), *The Warriors* (Jove, 1985)

We deliberately divide our time between Connecticut and South Carolina. Since I don't ski, living in an all-weather climate eleven-plus months of the year is important, because there's no tranquilizer made that can beat a half hour of good exercise. I am not a jock, but I swim regularly, and walk vigorously for a half hour or more three times a week—jogging for stretches along the way. I find this relaxes me and totally clears my mind. So do nine holes of golf (I can't abide playing 18), but I have less chance to fit in the necessary time.

Every year or so, I take a special holiday and either direct a theater piece with an amateur group, or act in one. I plunge completely into the work for four-six weeks and become revitalized. This is not entirely separate from my writing though. In contact with live audiences, I soak up reactions to material written by others. The experience teaches a lot about such things as exposition and dialogue. For relaxation I'd rate theater work one step "below" exercise, since part of my mind's working even while I'm relaxing.

I read extensively; for relaxation, I always choose something impractical. That is, in no way related to current work.

And I find travel to other parts of the world (or even the next town) great for unwinding. At some pain, I've learned not to confuse business travel, pleasant as it may be, with vacations worthy of the name. I need at least a week in another place, doing nothing "practical," to slow down; others tell me they do, too. Three-day weekends are fun, but don't do much to brake a racing thought process, since I'm usually racing to get home at the end.

. . . . .

Henry Kissinger
▲▲▲▲▲▲▲▲▲▲▲▲▲▲▲▲▲▲▲▲▲▲

Policy adviser; author, *Challenges of Change* (Public Affairs Press, 1971), *The White House Years* (Little, Brown, 1979), *Years of Upheaval* (Little, Brown, 1982)

Reading murder mysteries.

. . . . .

Norman Podhoretz
▲▲▲▲▲▲▲▲▲▲▲▲▲▲▲▲▲▲▲▲▲▲▲▲▲▲▲

Editor, *Commentary*

The main thing I do to relax is listen to music (classical) on my stereo system. I also read, go to the movies, and watch television, depending on my mood. On certain rare occasions when I have enough time, I like driving around the country, especially the West and the Southwest.

· · · · ·

Kim Hunter
Actress

Mostly I read books, go to the theater and concerts, walk, enjoy friends, and cook. Also, after all these years of puttering, I'm taking piano lessons. When I'm not working, the more improvisatory my life is, the happier I am. The demands of the work are so structured, and all-consuming, time without pressure is necessary to recoup and refresh.

· · · · ·

John Devaney
Editor; author, *Great Sports Stars of Yesteryear, Where Are They Today* (Crown, 1985), *Winners of the Heisman Trophy* (Walker, 1986), *Lyndon Johnson, President* (Walker, 1986)

As the saying goes, the difference between men and boys is that men play with more expensive toys. In my case, the toys are recording equipment that enables me to tape broadcasts and old 78-rpm records of swing and jazz music of the 1940s. One reason why I bought the car that I now drive was that it has a tape deck in it and the other car I was considering did not. I dislike the long drive—about a hundred miles—that my family and I make most weekends to our country place. I've often felt that whatever relaxation I had enjoyed in the country was wiped out by the exhausting time being caught in traffic jams during our return. Now, playing my tapes by Glenn Miller, Benny Goodman et al, I forget the waits in traffic by enjoying the same toys that help me get away from work during the week.

· · · · ·

Jim Borgman

Political cartoonist

My leisure activities are rather uncolorful, I'm afraid. I work on our house (we've fixed up two now, just a tad short of rehabbing in both cases). I take walks and stare into space a lot. I play with my little boy, mostly trying to get his electric train back on its track. I read a lot, but that is pretty much an extension of my work.

I've become convinced in the last year that a big part of creativity involves fallow time for the mind. I no longer feel that I must always be "doing" something. My mind requires lots of solitude and quiet time to put its haphazard impressions together.

· · · · ·

Sandy Richman

Stuntwoman

I bought a 1790 rowhouse in New Hope, Pennsylvania, and redid the inside completely. I ripped out everything except the overhead beams and hardwood floors. I stripped the kitchen cabinets and painted the whole house myself. I had new plumbing and electrical wiring installed.

I wouldn't want to move out of New York but the house is a great place to go to get away from the City for a while. I love it. I can drive down in the morning and come back late in the afternoon. And sometimes I go down there on weekends.

I'm also writing a book—an action thriller, with a woman as a star for a change, instead of Rambo.

. . . . .

James A. McDivitt

Astronaut, *Apollo* 9; executive vice president, Defense Electronics Operations, Rockwell International Corp.

Leisure should be an important part of any executive's schedule, but I'm sure that many of us just allow it to happen without the proper amount of planning or structure. I personally enjoy getting outdoors to hike, camp, and hunt. And, although it may be drudgery to some, yard work is leisure for me and seeing the results of my labor gives me a great deal of satisfaction.

. . . . .

Rona Jaffe

Author, *Mr. Right Is Dead* (Dell, 1980), *Mazes & Monsters* (Dell, 1982), *Away From Home* (Dell, 1982)

For a novelist, everything is potential material, even if it doesn't seem so at the time. Reading, travel, seeing movies, talking with friends, just being alone to let my mind wander, can help ideas and solve problems. I like to walk around and look at people and places, and try to imagine the people's lives.

. . . . .

Alexander Cohen

Theatrical and television producer

I take June and July off. I go to France. It takes me about two weeks to unwind, during which time I talk to New York about five or six times a day. But after those two weeks, it somehow all disappears.

· · · · ·

John J. Curley

President, chief operating officer, Gannett Co., Inc.

I run and ride my bike because they can be done in a wide variety of places and can be worked into the schedule fairly easily.

· · · · ·

Judith Crist

Theater and movie critic

I'm hard put to answer any question about my leisure. After all, my professional life as a critic is devoted to films and theater—to which most people devote their leisure. My leisure—relaxing and getting away from it all—is spent with flesh-and-blood friends, in listening to classical music and in reading (with the emphasis on mysteries). These activities refresh me for the voyeurism of my profession—and do supplement my critical interests.

· · · · ·

Beverly Sills

General director, New York City Opera Company

I do crossword puzzles and jigsaw puzzles, and in the summer I fish—no phones, no music, nothing—just me and my casting rod.

· · · · ·

Jane Meara

Author, *Growing Up Catholic* (Doubleday, 1986); Associate editor, Beech Tree Books (William Morrow & Co.)

I garden a lot, at least in the summertime. We have both a flower and vegetable garden. I find it completely relaxing. It wipes everything out of my mind.

I also knit or read. In fact, when I have free time, one of the big decisions I always must make is whether I'm going to knit or to read.

I'm not the kind of person who can sit still for very long. I love TV. I have the television set on a lot, but I can't just sit and look at it. I have to be doing something. So I knit. Then I feel I'm accomplishing something.

. . . . .

Isaac Asimov
Author

People expect to hear that I take a slug of booze, listen to rock, or go up on the roof and sunbathe. But I write! That's how I relax. For me, "work" is *not* being busy at the typewriter.

. . . . .

Jeane Dixon
Spiritualist

I do not nor do I want to "get away from it all." Rather than getting away from it all, I relish staying with it, conquering it, and moving on to the next challenge.

I believe that work is prayer and love in action. Approached that way, any task becomes ennobling. We need not be compulsive about our work to take delight in it and see in its completion the fulfillment of God's plan for us as individuals.

True happiness and peace comes from finding our mission and purpose in life. When we discover that, and pursue it, we do not tire nor become discouraged. Each new morning is a reborn world in which all our work can serve the Lord who has given it to us.

. . . . .

Sammy Cahn

Lyricist

I am one of those rare but totally happy people who have found that work is play. I relax and get away from it all by doing what I do, which is rhyming words for pleasure—and PROFIT.

I am always at the typemachine. I am always most comfortable when I am seated in front of it, and always at my most relaxed! I have made it a rule never to sit down UNLESS it is all "set to go," so to speak.

People who have watched me think it is some kind of miracle, and I'm happy to report it *is* some kind of miracle, because I often sit back and sort of watch my fingers go at it!

. . . . .

John S. Bull

Astronaut

My leisure-time activities have been greatly influenced by my family, and generally separated from my professional activities. Over the past fifteen years, as my two children have grown into teenagers, my leisure-time activities have been greatly involved with their many activities.

My family has been very outdoors oriented; hiking, camping, boating, swimming, water-skiing, and snow skiing are some typical family activities.

In addition, my wife and I take great pride in watching and sometimes participating with our children in their activities such as football, basketball, baseball, softball, golf, soccer, dancing, and cheerleading.

When I find it necessary to get away from it all and relax, I thoroughly enjoy the therapy of jogging about three miles a day. I also enjoy construction projects, large ones, such as adding a room to the house.

. . . . .

Patricia Neal
Actress

In my few spare days, especially in the summer, I love relaxing in my house on Martha's Vineyard, reading, seeing friends and family and walking in my yard admiring the roses and lilies. In New York, I love watching the tugboats and freighters pass by my window on the East River. It is so beautiful and relaxing. It's almost as if I could reach out and touch them, or hop aboard and sail away to some great adventure . . . all in my mind anyway, for time is so precious and rushes by so quickly, the next thing I know, I'm off on a plane to this place or that.

. . . . .

Pete Seeger
Folk singer

I tend to be too busy. However, when I am out on tour, I seize whatever few seconds I can find to relax, either in an airplane or a waiting room, or simply lying down on the floor backstage for 10 minutes and breathing deeply.

I guess breathing deeply and thinking good thoughts is really pretty basic, no matter what words you use to describe it.

Of course, for many of us, the time comes when we have to bite the bullet and decide not to do some job which is causing us too much stress or leaving some situation which we can't handle.

. . . . .

Walter Cronkite
Television journalist

To relax, I sail for a couple of hours or a couple of weeks; the longer I sail, the greater the release.

. . . . .

Kathy Keeton
President, *Omni* magazine; author, *Woman of Tomorrow* (St. Martin, 1985)

I have two favorite ways to get away from it all, in addition to the time I spend exercising. I spend time with my dogs, and I take short holidays whenever possible. Though they are not so out of the ordinary escapes, they are invaluable to me. Years ago I acquired a prize-winning Rhodesian Ridgeback. They are really quite unique and I couldn't resist the temptation to breed more. Currently, I have four Ridgebacks, and soon hope to have another. I love the special time spent grooming, feeding and walking these magnificent animals.

As for vacations, my favorite spots are South Africa and Italy. I travel there at least once a year. The phones don't ring and there's a certain amount of anonymity that I can't find in New York. Things seem more accessible, and I do a great deal of shopping. During my last trip to Verona and Venice, for example, I went on a furniture buying spree which netted seventy pieces of Italian Renaissance furniture.

. . . . .

Vance Bourjaily
Author, *The Unnatural Enemy* (University of Arizona, 1984), *Confessions of a Spent Youth* (Arbor House, 1986)

I like to hunt mushrooms, fish for trout, cook stuff, play with dogs
. . . sleep. And many other things, all of them limited by time,
money and the demands made by less congenial things which apparently must be done.

A FINAL WORD

You *can* make changes in your life that will enable you to do more
in less time and achieve a sense of self-worth. You *can* learn to shed
the stress your professional life often produces. You *can* find the
means of energizing and enriching the hours you spend away from
your job.

The first step is to reexamine your ambitions and goals and
make them more clear-cut. Next, you have to establish a system
of priorities for achieving those goals. You have to get control of
your discretionary time, not allow it to be dissipated by the demands of others. You have to learn to delegate and make up your
mind to conquer procrastination.

You have to begin now. Today. The commitments and pressures of your job are not temporary—despite what you keep telling
yourself. What may seem temporary has a way of becoming permanent.

Once you're on the road, you'll find the rewards go beyond
greater achievement and better performance. You'll begin deriving
new excitement from your career. You'll boost your self-esteem
and the recognition you get from others. You'll come to derive a
fuller sense of pleasure and satisfaction from your work and life.

Index